Speaking the Unspeakable

Homosexuality — A Biblical and Modern Perspective

Richard D. Starr

NORTHWESTERN PUBLISHING HOUSE
Milwaukee, Wisconsin

Scripture taken from the
HOLY BIBLE, NEW INTERNATIONAL VERSION.
Copyright © 1973, 1978, 1984, International Bible Society.
Used by permission of Zondervan Bible Publishers.

Library of Congress Card 86-63850
Northwestern Publishing House
1250 N. 113th St., P.O. Box 26975, Milwaukee, WI 53226-0975
© 1987 by Northwestern Publishing House.
Published 1987
Printed in the United States of America
ISBN 0-8100-0259-0

SPECIAL THANKS

to the members of
Shepherd of Peace Evangelical
Lutheran Church
Worthington, Ohio
for granting me the time
to research and write this book;

to my friends, Phil and Karen McCoy,
for encouraging me,
and for their editorial help and equipment;

and to my parents, John and Marie Starr,
for teaching me to love
all people for Jesus' sake
and for his sake never
to compromise God's Word.

CONTENTS

1. Speaking of Homosexuality   1
2. The Old Testament Speaks
   of Homosexuality   9
3. The New Testament Speaks
   of Homosexuality   19
4. Further New Testament Passages
   Speaking of Homosexuality   27
5. Society Speaks of Homosexuality   37
6. Christian Churches Speak
   of Homosexuality   44
7. Speaking of the Cause of Homosexuality   58
8. Speaking of the Cure for Homosexuality   63
9. Speaking of AIDS   71
   Notes   79
   Appendixes   80
   Glossary of Homosexual Terms   85

1. SPEAKING OF HOMOSEXUALITY

A TIMELY TOPIC

Why a book on homosexuality? Isn't it a cut and dried issue in the Scriptures? Besides, homosexuality deals with a very small portion of society. Certainly no one I know would ever be involved in such a thing! I've been in the parish ministry for twenty years and never had a homosexual in my congregation.

You may be thinking some of these thoughts. Yet, for some reason you've picked up this book and have started reading it. It may be out of simple curiosity. It may be that you're just looking for some information on a subject about which you know very little. It may be that you are greatly troubled. Regardless of your motivation, let me ask you a question or two before going any further. Think about your answers carefully and be honest — you are the only one who will know how you answered, but you may not be the only one who will benefit from those answers and this book.

What would you do if your son or daughter, nephew or niece, or even your spouse suddenly told you that he or she were "gay"? How would you respond to the following people if they were to move next door to you, come to you for counseling, or join your congregation? Would you recoil from them in revulsion, pretend they didn't exist, or even tell them to "get out and stay out" until they changed their ways?

Meet Christopher Hawks from New Jersey:

> I am seventeen years old, a senior in high school, and openly gay. Homosexuality had always been a major force in the shaping of my life and personality. Learning to be myself, and to like myself, has been a continuous growing experience; one that is still going on.... The best thing that came from my move was that I was now close to a big city. The city is wonderful! There are so many gays everywhere. It used to make me feel so good to go into the city and see them all living openly and happily, and it gave me strength to be myself.[1]

Consider James Brock, a twenty-four year old, from Seattle, Washington. James had been concerned about the Scripture's prohibitions against homosexuality all his life until he met a "wise and wonderful pastor."

> The most difficult problem created by my homosexuality was to deal with the religious beliefs I was raised with.... My religious roots are both Pentecostal and Baptist.... I tried to change myself. I prayed everyday to have a sexual feeling for girls. I prayed that I would start liking sports. I prayed that I would stop watching sports just so I could look at the guys. But no change came.... Religion had been my lifeline, my stronghold, the one thing I was good at.... A very wise and wonderful pastor opened my eyes, and helped me reopen my heart. Together he and I read the Scriptures which had plagued my life. He pointed out that each of them could be read to say what anyone wanted it to say. He showed me how beliefs differed from religion to religion.... As he said, I had been given life by God, and these feelings were a part of the whole me that God had created.... It was such a relief to know that I could be a Christian who was gay.[2]

What would you have told eighteen year old Mark Maki from Minnesota if you had been the Lutheran friend or pastor he turned to for help?

> I am deaf, gay, and eighteen years old. I grew up in a small town and attended the Minnesota School for the Deaf. I

was seventeen when I first realized that I was gay. . . . One Sunday, I went to the Lutheran Church for the Deaf. After the service was over, I decided to talk to the pastor and I told her I was gay. She understood, and told me about this lesbian couple she knew. . . . They have made me very happy . . . they said that many pastors make gays feel bad and guilty. I then prayed to God to accept me as a gay person. I found out that God does accept and love me as his child. . . . Now I am at St. Mary's Junior College in Minneapolis and am very excited to have gay friends.[3]

Isolated incidents? Perhaps, but probably not. These accounts were taken from a book entitled *One Teenager in Ten*, implying that ten percent of the world's population is homosexual or at least would be without laws and social repression against homosexuality.

The church has always been a formidable force in keeping homosexuality in check, but that, too, is changing. As we shall see later in this book, every major denomination of Christianity is being affected and many are changing centuries-old positions on homosexuality. Perhaps most alarming is that this change is being led by seminary professors and the clergy. "I am a child of God, a man, a homosexual, a Christian, a Lutheran — in that order — and I am a husband committed to my wife, who knows I'm gay." The author of this statement is a thirty-three year old Lutheran minister serving a Midwestern parish! Although this pro-homosexual trend is currently changing for many Lutherans, such is not the case for the Wisconsin Evangelical Lutheran Synod in which I am a pastor.

Homosexuality is a subject which demands the attention of every concerned pastor and lay person today. It won't simply go away and it would be wrong (although convenient) to ignore it. Faithful shepherds under Christ must be prepared to give counsel and aid to their flock in this area. Dedicated lay people must be prepared to respond in an appropriate and Christian manner to the person caught in the sin of homosexuality. Although I have been in the parish ministry for only five years, during that time one man, one woman, one teenage boy and one teenage girl have come to me for help in wrestling with the matter of homosexuality. Five families in my small mission congregation have spoken to me concerning relatives, friends, co-workers or classmates who are openly homosexual. I'm sure some of you have had similar experiences. If not, you probably will. Therefore, it is vitally important that we be well prepared to give an answer to the questions that may be asked concerning homosexuality and that we be absolutely certain that we answer from God's Word correctly.

DEFINING HOMOSEXUALITY

Webster defines homosexuality in this way, "of, relating to, or exhibiting sexual desire toward a member of one's own sex." For our purposes, we shall add to desire "behavior." Homosexuality refers to overt sexual relations or emotional attachment involving sexual attraction between individuals — male or female — of the same sex. Certainly homosexuality does not describe a person's physical appearance or mannerisms. Effeminate traits in a man or masculine traits in a woman do not identify either as homosexual.

Homosexuality, as a condition or state of being, is found only in human beings. Although some animal studies indicate that some higher mammals display at least partial homosexuality from time to time, no animal species has ever displayed exclusive homosexuality in which one animal could be classified as purely homosexual, preferring sexual relations only with a member of its own sex. Homosexual behavior occurs in animals *only* when heterosexual relations are impossible. Exclusive homosexuality is a purely human phenomenon. Of course, we do not turn to the animal kingdom for our moral standards or for a determination of what is sinful and what is not.

The sin of homosexuality has undoubtedly been present in this world for a very long time. It can be found in the history of almost every land and culture. However, it is certain that God did not create Adam and Eve as homosexuals. ("For this reason a man will leave his father and mother and be united to his wife, and they will become one flesh" Genesis 2:24.) Although sin has been with us since the Fall, the sin of homosexuality has been with us since early on — but *not* from the very start of things.

It is important to note that much of the scientific world considers homosexuality to be an unchosen and natural state of being.

There is much debate and indecision among scientists and behaviorists as to the cause of homosexuality. Yet homosexuality is seldom seen for what it really is: a sin which can trap and enslave the perpetrator, in much the same way that the abuse of alcohol can lead to the sinful enslavement of alcoholism. When a person reaches the point with homosexuality that an alcoholic does with alcohol, then, he or she *is* a homosexual. This is not a popular view with homosexuals who prefer to rationalize by blaming their sin on someone else, such as parents, society or even God.

Supposedly, homosexuals are constitutionally different from heterosexuals. At the same time their proponents most often stress the similarities with heterosexuals in an attempt to dispel homophobia — the fear of or hatred toward homosexuals and homosexuality. Pro-homosexual writers stress the fact that the only difference between homosexuals and heterosexuals is that homosexuals predominantly prefer members of their own sex as objects of sexual desire while heterosexuals predominantly prefer members of the opposite sex for such purposes. Many writers further try to minimize the differences between heterosexuals and homosexuals by classifying all people as more or less bisexual — sexually attracted to members of either sex — stressing that the only difference is "sexual preference" — a preference for one sex or the other for most of their lives. So, while insisting that homosexuals are constitutionally different, pro-homosexual writers also contend that we are all alike. This circular logic is like having your cake and eating it too. And we all know that just isn't possible.

Regardless of the cause or rationale, homosexuality is simply the sexual desire and/or behavior toward a member or members of one's own sex. A homosexual is a person — male or female — who gains sexual and emotional gratification by engaging in that desire and/or behavior.

Another characteristic of homosexuality is promiscuity. While a very few homosexuals, usually those of middle age or older, practice sexual faithfulness to only one partner, the vast majority of homosexuals eagerly seek out one sexual partner after another. They may have a dozen or more anonymous sexual encounters in a single night at a homosexual bath house or adult book store equipped with waist high "glory holes" between individual video booths.

This was verified by a young man whom I met while researching this book. He had been reared in an American Lutheran Church parsonage. In college he had become involved in homosexual activities. He had hundreds of sexual encounters in those four years by his own estimation. Then, partly because he felt God required faithfulness of the homosexual and partly because he had fallen in love with one man, he settled down with one sexual partner for three years. That relationship dissolved when both of the young men became bored with each other and wanted other sexual partners. After one and a half years of promiscuous playing of the field, he settled down again with another man. This relationship did not last even two years. The man is now, by his own admission, looking for homosexual partners wherever and whenever he can. He still believes God requires his children to be faithful to only one partner, whether they are heterosexual or homosexual. Yet he realizes that he cannot be faithful to just one man and therefore he feels he cannot be a child of God either. He insists that the best homosexual sex is anonymous, impersonal, promiscuous and public: toilets, parks, beaches, elevators, cars, cabs, buses, subways, alleys, department stores, offices, super-markets and theaters. He assured me that he has committed homosexual acts in all of those places. He told me that he knows of no homosexual men or women who remain faithful to one sexual partner in the same way that many heterosexual couples remain faithful to each other. Promiscuity is definitely typical of homosexuality.

The gravity of homosexuality in today's society gives thoughtful people another reason to study this entire matter in some detail. The sins of homosexuality, incest and pedophilia (sexual child abuse) have become epidemic prior to the fall of almost every civilization known to man. Only limited exposure to the evening news, prime time television or the morning paper quickly confirms that all three of these sins are epidemic in the United States of America today.

HOW THE SCRIPTURES
SPEAK OF HOMOSEXUALITY

An entirely new attitude toward homosexuality has arisen within the Christian church during the last two or three decades. Lying at the very heart of the matter are the principles of Bible interpretation. Broadly speaking, biblical interpretation among believers exists on a line between two opposite ends.

On the one end are those who say that the Bible means what it says. No ifs. No ands. No buts. The Bible says that God created the world in six days — that's the way it happened. The Bible says the Red Sea parted — it parted. The Bible says Jonah spent three days in the belly of a great fish — it is certainly so. This is the belief about God's Word which is followed in this book — that the Bible is God's Word and that it means what it says.

No one should ever feel obligated to apologize for taking a stand at this end of the biblical interpretation line, for truth can abide no compromise. Scripture tells us in no uncertain terms what homosexuality is, from where it comes, and how it takes over the minds and lives of people. Scripture also tells us how to escape its vicious grasp. Therefore it is appropriate that we carefully study what God tells us through his Word. Accepting God's instruction without condition, we must be careful to say nothing less and nothing more than he himself has said.

Toward the other end of the Bible interpretation line are those who insist that the Bible must be interpreted with the aid of the tools of textual and historical criticism. The Bible, they argue, was set in writing by men, conditioned by their cultures, using the literary conventions of their times. To get at the truth of the Scriptures, they say, it is necessary to understand and peel away those cultural and stylistic aspects. Unfortunately, this is the stand taken by the majority of Lutherans today. Many Lutheran seminary students are being taught that they should interpret biblical texts by applying their human reason and prejudices to the text and that the meaning of Scripture changes for each generation. This is certainly not letting God speak clearly to us from his Word. Rather, it is putting words — the words of sinful human beings — into his inerrant holy mouth.

While it's obvious that we do not agree with such people on what Scripture is or on its validity, we cannot simply leave it at that. It is necessary that we review what Scripture does say about homosexuality and become thoroughly familiar with the manner in which the Scriptures are wrongfully used to excuse, promote and rationalize homosexuality.

The reason this is so essential to all of us is familiar. Undoubtedly, each of us must struggle with some particular weakness or pet sin. We all know from personal experience how skilled the unholy three — the devil, the world, and our own sinful flesh — are at tempting us to fall repeatedly into that sin. Rationalization is a great weapon in that attack. If an individual's particular weakness is the sin of homosexuality, we can be sure that the person will reach out and latch onto anything that tells him it is not a sin or, at least, not nearly so bad a sin as he might previously have been taught to believe, as though a "little sin" were less damning than a "big sin." Such rationalization is exhibited in the accounts of James and Mark, the homosexuals quoted at the beginning of this book.

2. THE OLD TESTAMENT SPEAKS OF HOMOSEXUALITY

GENESIS 19

The account of Sodom and Gomorrah is probably the best known and certainly the most compelling passage in the Old Testament condemning homosexual behavior. So well-known was Sodom's sin that the term sodomy is now attributed to certain homosexual acts. Since the account is so familiar, we shall not go into great detail retelling the circumstances of that tragic event. However, by way of review, we read verses four through nine:

> Before they had gone to bed, all the men from every part of the city of Sodom — both young and old — surrounded the house. They called to Lot, "Where are the men who came to you tonight? Bring them out to us so that we can have sex with them." Lot went outside to meet them and shut the door behind him and said, "No, my friends. Don't do this wicked thing. Look, I have two daughters who have never slept with a man. Let me bring them out to you, and you can do what you like with them. But don't do anything to these

men, for they have come under the protection of my roof." "Get out of our way," they replied. And they said, "This fellow came here as an alien, and now he wants to play the judge! We'll treat you worse than them." They kept bringing pressure on Lot and moved forward to break down the door.

It would be difficult to find a more terrible account anywhere in God's Word. The description of their horribly lewd behavior, as well as the sudden and complete destruction of Sodom and Gomorrah later in Genesis 19, are meant to shock us by their blunt and gruesome details. Dr. Martin Luther confessed that he had difficulty simply reading the chapter (*es geht mir durch mein ganzes Herz* — it goes through my entire heart).

The proportions to which the vice of the men of Sodom had grown is indicated by the fact that "both young and old" gathered at the house of Lot for sexual gratification. Homosexuality had permeated the city. This is unmistakably clear by the two phrases "all the men" and "from every part of the city."

The Hebrew verb, *ned'ah*, translated as "that we may know them" in the King James Version (KJV) and as "so that we can have sex with them" in the NIV, is not used out of delicacy or shame on their part. So blatant was their homosexuality that they shouted their sexual desires aloud, clamoring in the streets of the city.

This behavior was used as an example of open and blatant sin in Isaiah 3:9: ". . . they parade their sin like Sodom; they do not hide it." In Judges 19:22 ("Bring out the man who came to your house so we can have sex with him"), this same verb *ned'ah* is used to describe the carnal sin of men having sex with boys. According to Leviticus 18:22 ("Do not lie with a man as one lies with a woman; that is detestable") and 20:23 ("You must not live according to the customs of the nations I am going to drive out before you. Because they did all these things, I abhorred them"), homosexuality was also very prevalent among the Canaanites. Romans 1:27 ("In the same way the men also abandoned natural relations with women and were inflamed with lust for one another") labels homosexuality a general characteristic of heathenism. There can be no doubt whatsoever that this Hebrew verb, "to know," is here to be understood "in the biblical sense," that is, to have sexual relationships.

Context makes it abundantly clear why the NIV has chosen to reflect that particular meaning in its translation. Anyone with the least spark of virtue and with any remains of natural light and conscience can see that the story of Sodom and Gomorrah speaks of homosexuality. It is obvious that homosexuality was accepted as normal behavior in Sodom. But acceptance didn't make it right or any less a sin. God's unusual and complete destruction of the city indicates that the people of Sodom had no remorse for their sin. It would have been bad enough if the Sodomites had practiced their sin in private, but they brought it out into the open and defied anyone to stop them.

Dr. Martin Luther knew of homosexuality, for in his day it was not all that rare. He also knew that the sin of Sodom and Gomorrah was homosexuality. In one of his lectures on Genesis 19, Luther tells us: "In Rome I saw some cardinals who were venerated as saints because they were satisfied with having intercourse with women."[4] The Reformer also had this to say about the sin of sodomy:

> The vice of the Sodomites is an unparalleled enormity. It departs from the natural passion and desire, planted into nature by God, according to which the male has a passionate desire for the female. Sodomy craves what is entirely contrary to nature. Whence comes this perversion? Without a doubt it comes from the devil. After a man has once turned aside from the fear of God, the devil puts such great pressure upon his nature that he extinguishes the fire of natural desire and stirs up another, which is contrary to nature.[5]

Luther pinpoints the cause of homosexuality — separation from God — and no matter how hard or long or loud a practicing, unrepentant homosexual cries, "Lord, Lord," he or she will not enter the kingdom of heaven, Matthew 7:21.

Before we move on from Genesis 19 and Luther, we should mention that Luther has been maligned for trying to vindicate the character of Lot, who offered his daughters for the men's sexual pleasure. Luther speculated that Lot was shrewd enough to know that the men would not want his daughters. So bent on satisfying their homosexual lust were they that his daughters were in no real danger. Yet, some have accused Luther of trying to promote the idea that one can avoid sin by sin. However, Luther is most clear on this point: "The principle that you may choose the lesser evil in order to avoid the greater is sound in external and physical affairs. But in spiritual relations it is different. You must never do evil so that good may come of it."[6]

In spite of the overwhelming clarity of the Sodom account in its condemnation of homosexuality, there are many interpreters of the Bible who ignore common sense and insist that the words must mean something other than what they say. Motivated by the desire to make sin legitimate for themselves and others, they offer their arguments in seemingly reasonable and convincing ways. They use all their persuasive powers to make their false biblical interpretations seem believable. This is especially damaging, because many religious leaders and scholars are leading the way in this abominable scratching of itching ears. They are twisting the Bible to make it say what people want to hear. Incredibly, they overlook the obvious and insist that Sodom's sin was not homosexuality but sacrifices to idols, pride and inhospitality!

Indeed, Scripture tells us these other sins were also prevalent in Sodom: "Hear the word of the Lord, you rulers of Sodom; listen to the law of our God, you people of Gomorrah! The multitude of your sacrifices — what are they to me? says the Lord" (Isaiah 1:10,11). "Now this was the sin of your sister Sodom: she and her daughters were arrogant, overfed and unconcerned; they did not help the poor and needy" (Ezekiel 16:49). "And among the prophets of Jerusalem I have seen something horrible: They commit adultery and live a lie. They strengthen the hands of evildoers, so that no one turns from his wickedness. They are all like Sodom to me; the people of Jerusalem are like Gomorrah" (Jeremiah 23:14). "If anyone will not welcome you or listen to your words, shake the dust off your feet when you leave that home or town. I tell you the truth, it will be more bearable for Sodom and Gomorrah on the day of judgment than for that town" (Matthew 10:14,15). "But when you enter a town and are not welcomed, go into its streets and say, 'Even the dust of your town that sticks to our feet we wipe off against you. Yet be sure of this: The kingdom of God is near.' I tell you, it will be more bearable on that day for Sodom than for that town" (Luke 10:10-12).

Obviously the ancient city of Sodom had fallen into numerous sins. Yet its most infamous sin was so well-known that it didn't need mentioning — indeed the very mention of the name

Sodom called to mind its sin of homosexuality. This fact is never mentioned by interpreters who seek to ignore the Bible's condemnation of the homosexuality in Sodom. At least some of these writers do concede that the account of Sodom and Gomorrah serves as a condemnation of homosexual *rape*.

John Boswell, in his book *Christianity, Social Tolerance, and Homosexuality* — the new "bible" of the homosexual community — proposes four reasons for the destruction of Sodom and Gomorrah: (1) because of their general wickedness; (2) because the men of the city tried to rape the angels; (3) because the men of the city tried to engage in homosexual intercourse with the angels; and (4) because of their inhospitable treatment of angels.

Boswell suggests the fourth reason as the main cause for the destruction of Sodom and Gomorrah. Boswell insists that all the men of Sodom, from the young to the old, gathered around Lot's house and demanded that the strangers be brought out to them for no other reason than to know who they were. He simplistically contends that the city was destroyed, not for sexual immorality, specifically homosexuality, but for the sin of inhospitality to strangers, in this case, a lack of respect for their privacy.

At times, Boswell and others add to their soup of misinterpretation the spice of confusion by not being as accurate as they might be with regard to scriptural facts. For example, the Hebrew verb "to know" is used eleven times in the Old Testament to refer to sexual intercourse, but Boswell says it is used in this way only ten times and that its use is insignificant. No word in God's holy Scripture is insignificant. Boswell also insists that it refers to homosexuality only once, but the truth is that both Genesis 19:5 ("They called to Lot, 'Where are the men who came to you tonight? Bring them out to us so that we can have sex with them.' ") and Judges 19:22 ("While they were enjoying themselves, some of the wicked men of the city surrounded the house. Pounding on the door, they shouted to the old man who owned the house, 'Bring out the man who came to your house so that we can have sex with him.' ") use it to refer to homosexual relations. Such action on the part of pro-homosexual writers lessens their credibility. Perhaps more damaging is the fact that the casual reader would probably not recognize this flagrant misrepresentation of the truth.

Boswell also points out that Jesus himself must have considered the sin of Sodom to be inhospitality, since he refers to it in that way when sending out seventy-two of his disciples:

> "But when you enter a town and are not welcomed, go into its streets and say, 'Even the dust of your town that sticks to our feet we wipe off against you. Yet be sure of this: The kingdom of God is near.' I tell you, it will be more bearable on that day for Sodom than for that town" (Luke 10:10-12).

Of course, the thought is not expressed by Boswell that because Sodom's sin of homosexuality and its punishment were so well known it became a benchmark by which all other punishments were judged. Therefore the two causes of punishment need not be related at all. But Boswell is extremely adept at turning his supposedly objective information into persuasive propaganda without it appearing as such to the casual or pro-homosexual reader.

Boswell would even have a person who has just read Genesis 19 believe that there is no sexual connotation at all in the account! He suggests that the men of Sodom did not have sexual gratification in mind as they banged on Lot's door. He insists that it was Lot who injected the idea of sex into the situation by offering his virgin daughters to the mob. Yet, one must ask why virgin daughters would satisfy the wants of these men if all they wanted was to satisfy their curiosity concerning the identity of the strangers? With this argument, Boswell betrays the bounds of "reason" he so passionately espouses.

Some other pro-homosexual writers are at least more honest in their presentations of the account, although still misguided in their conclusions. They freely admit that the Genesis 19 account clearly speaks of the men of the city wanting to have sexual relationships with the two angels disguised as men. However, they contend that the sin was not in the *wanting* but in the *forcing*. They insist that the account can be used only against homosexual rape and not against consenting homosexual acts.

In conclusion, the Genesis 19 account of Sodom and Gomorrah is seen by pro-homosexual writers and proponents as being at most, a condemnation of homosexual desire that is linked with aggression and at the least, a condemnation of poor manners and inhospitality. In their opinion, it has nothing whatsoever to do with homosexuality as a condition or homosexual acts between consenting persons. Through the power of the Holy Spirit, God's children know differently. To follow the reasoning of the pro-homosexual writers would be the same as failing to condemn a murderer for killing in a fit of rage. The rage does not make the murder any less a murder.

GENESIS 38:8-10

Then Judah said to Onan, "Lie with your brother's wife and fulfill your duty to her as a brother-in-law to produce offspring for your brother." But Onan knew that the offspring would not be his; so whenever he lay with his brother's wife, he spilled his seed on the ground to keep from producing offspring for his brother. What he did was wicked in the Lord's sight; so he put him to death also.

The Onan account, of course, does not deal with homosexuality or even sins of a sexual nature at all, although it has wrongfully been used by some people to condemn masturbation. But pro-homosexual writers have used this account to explain why homosexuality and other non-procreative acts such as intercourse with a menstruating woman were banned by law. They suggest that the deliberate and non-procreative spilling of semen was considered to be the same as the deliberate destruction of human life. Such spilling of semen occurs in male masturbation, male homosexual acts, and in coitus interruptus, which they erroneously designate as the sin of Onan.

As can be seen in verse 10, Onan was punished for his defiant rejection of God's will; it had nothing to do with sexuality or even procreation. So in combating the pro-homosexual presentation, be prepared for the false accusation that all of Israel's laws were designed simply to help the nation grow into "numbers as numerous as the stars in the sky or the sand on the shore." Now that this objective is no longer of prime importance, it is said that such rules no longer apply.

LEVITICUS 18:22; 20:13

Do not lie with a man as one lies with a woman; that is detestable.

If a man lies with a man as one lies with a woman, both of them have done what is detestable. They must be put to death; their blood will be on their own heads.

We must realize that these prohibitions against homosexuality are a part of the Levitical law code which is, for the most part, no longer binding on New Testament Christians. As St. Paul asserted, "Do not let anyone judge you by what you eat or drink, or with regard to a religious festival, a new moon celebration or a Sabbath day" (Colossians 2:16). Unfortunately, confusion often arises between the moral law contained in Leviticus and the Levitical law code, since much of moral law is interspersed in the Levitical law code.

The moral law stated within these passages is part of the Lord's continuing will for his people and is binding for all time. Unlawful sexual relations are against God's will for all people, for all time. In Old Testament times the punishment for such crimes was usually most severe — death. Pro-homosexual writers discount the Leviticus passages for the most part because of the death penalty along with other prohibitions that are no longer binding. Although they agree that the Old Testament demanded the death penalty for those committing homosexual acts, they also insist that if one is going to use the Old Testament to condemn homosexuality, then one must be consistent and demand the death penalty today for homosexuals. Their argument here is that no one would be so barbaric as to suggest the death penalty for homosexuals or homosexual behavior today so, therefore, the law must no longer apply. Such a line of reasoning comes closer to rationalization than logic — much like the tail wagging the dog.

(It might be noted here that until fairly recent times, homosexuals *were* often put to death and earned the name "faggots" while burning at the stake. A faggot refers to the lower dead branches of coniferous trees which are mostly worthless for sustaining useful fires and were used to fuel the fires of persons burned at the stake.)

Others suggest that the passages in Leviticus condemn the homosexual *act* but not the state of *being* a homosexual — again faulty logic. That's similar to giving a child a piece of candy but telling him not to eat it. These people obviously do not realize that sin begins with thoughts contrary to God's will and that sin is more than merely the act. The Lord says, "Man looks at the outward appearance, but the Lord looks at the heart" (1 Samuel 16:7).

Since homosexuality and incest were rampant among the heathen nations who were separated from God by their unbelief, some pro-homosexual writers promote the ideas that the prohibitions against such vices were put in place merely to keep Israel separate and distinct as a people from the other nations.

The Hebrew word, to'ebah, translated as "detestable" in these Leviticus passages, is also used in Deuteronomy 32:16 ("They made him jealous with their foreign gods and angered him with their detestable idols") and Isaiah 44:19 ("Shall I make a detestable thing from what is left? Shall I bow down to a block of wood?"). These other passages refer to false gods and idols, the worship of which is intrinsically evil, violating the First Commandment. Of course, using the helter-skelter logic of these writers it is convenient to forget that when wanting to see only one side of an issue.

TEMPLE PROSTITUTION
AND OTHER EXAMPLES

"No Israelite man or woman is to become a temple prostitute" (Deuteronomy 23:17).
"There were even male shrine prostitutes in the land; the people engaged in all the detestable practices of the nations the Lord had driven out before the Israelites" (1 Kings 14:24).
"He [good king Asa] expelled the male shrine prostitutes from the land and got rid of all the idols his father had made" (1 Kings 15:12).
"He [good king Jehoshaphat] rid the land of the rest of the male shrine prostitutes who remained there even after the reign of his father Asa" (1 Kings 22:46).

All of these passages speak of male and/or female temple prostitution. It is well known that male temple prostitutes service both males and females in their despicable and perverted worship practices. While the verses should not be used by themselves as a condemnation of homosexual behavior, it is significant that male prostitution seems to be singled out for special revulsion in the eyes of God and his people. This seems to be the tenor of 1 Kings 14:24, for example, "There were *even* male shrine prostitutes in the land."

The pro-homosexual writers use these passages, however, to try to show that God didn't actually condemn homosexuality. According to these writers, homosexuality and male prostitution were supposedly rejected as proper behavior for the Israelites *only* because they were identified with the worship of idols.

Of course, pro-homosexual writers do not stop at merely trying to debunk the clear passages of the Old Testament condemning homosexuality. Without any scriptural substantiation, they try to show that there were intense, homosexual love relationships in the Old Testament. They cite Saul and David as an example of this, suggesting that Saul's anger with David was fueled by David's rejection of Saul as a lover for the more desirable body of Saul's son, Jonathan. David and Jonathan as well as Naomi and Ruth are also used as examples of homosexual couples.

Ecclesiastical and secular literature of the Middle Ages alludes to the strong and faithful friendships of these godly people and at times suggests erotic overtones. Yet the Middle Ages were probably no more moral or immoral than the present age. Sinners still tried to call sin something other than what it was, just as sinners do today. Yesterday, today and tomorrow the argumentation is faulty, although it may be appealing to someone looking for an excuse to make a sin acceptable.

As children grow up, one of the first rationalizations they learn is: Everyone else is doing it so it must be all right for me to do it, too. This type of argument is employed — and just as wrongly — by the pro-homosexual writers. They point out that the ancient heathen world was not opposed to homosexuality. Even pro-homosexual writers who claim to be Christian insist that since the Romans found nothing wrong with homosexuality, God's inerrant word must be in error with its clear prohibitions against it. One would not expect the heathen Roman of old to understand God's words, "for they are foolishness to him and he cannot understand them, because they are spiritually discerned" (1 Corinthians 2:14). The fact remains that a Christian certainly cannot use the Roman's heathen beliefs as justification for behavior which opposes the clear and explicit will of God.

3. THE NEW TESTAMENT SPEAKS OF HOMOSEXUALITY

JESUS' ATTITUDE

Turning to the New Testament, we find the same methods of Bible interpretation employed by those advocating homosexuality. Much is made of the fact that Jesus did not specifically condemn homosexuality. Anyone who uses passages penned by the Apostle Paul is termed a "Paulist" as opposed to a Christian. Apparently, if Jesus said it, then it must be so, but if one of God's inspired writers penned the words, he is immediately suspect. The argument is put forth that if homosexuality were really a serious sin, Jesus would certainly never have allowed it to go by unmentioned and unnoticed. Never mind that the New Testament strongly and plainly condemns homosexuality. Because Jesus himself did not specifically condemn it, pro-homosexual advocates suggest it must be permissible.

It is that very attitude which prompted the assignment and writing of a conference paper and finally this book. While attending a seminar on "The Scriptures and Human Sexuality" at Trinity Lutheran Seminary, Columbus, Ohio, I was teamed with an American Lutheran Church (ALC) pastor, his wife, and three Roman Catholic nuns. In the course of working on a hypothetical problem we had been given to solve, the ALC pastor said that the Sixth Commandment applied only to married people and that there were no prohibitions in the New Testament against sexual activity among the unmarried. When I quoted Matthew 5:28, "But I tell you that anyone who looks at a woman lustfully has already committed adultery with her in his heart," one of the nuns questioned whether or not we could be sure that Jesus had really said those words!

Here is a case where even if Jesus said it, if it doesn't fit into their wishes, it is permissible to dismiss Christ's teaching as possibly being added many years later by misguided moralists. These people with whom I attended the seminar were not detached writers and scholars, but everyday people with the responsibility to deal with and guide God's people. Yet they echoed the thoughts and musings of men rather than those of the Lord.

The pro-homosexual writers insist that Jesus was indifferent to sexuality of all kinds, that he did not condemn the practice of sexual intercourse among the unmarried, and that he never even remotely spoke of homosexuality. As far as sexuality was concerned, Jesus was only interested in faithfulness. But Jesus spoke the words of Matthew 15:19, "For out of the heart come evil thoughts, murder, adultery, sexual immorality, theft, false testimony, slander." Certainly, adultery and sexual immorality are not limiting; they refer to any sexual behavior among the married and the unmarried.

Nor is Jesus Christ himself immune from the same accusation made of Saul, David, Jonathan, Naomi and Ruth in the Old Testament. Just as some have suggested Paul's thorn in the flesh was homosexuality, they have cast the same aspersions on our Savior. The relationship of Jesus and John, the disciple whom "Jesus loved," is cited as evidence that Jesus perhaps engaged in homosexual activity himself. They note that Jesus only had special relationships with men. While it is true that Jesus had special close friends in Peter, James and John, he was also close friends with Mary Magdalene and Mary and Martha of Bethany. When a person has convinced himself that his sin is acceptable, what better way to convince others than to suggest that Jesus did not consider the activity a sin at all but even participated in it himself!

> Because of this, God gave them over to shameful lusts. Even their women exchanged natural relations for unnatural ones. In the same way the men also abandoned natural relations with women and were inflamed with lust for one another. Men committed indecent acts with other men, and received in themselves the due penalty for their perversion.

Chapter one of Romans is a description of the godless world — strikingly applicable at all times and especially, it seems, at the zenith of so-called "intellectual enlightenment." It is a description of what happens when people deliberately transfer the honor due to God, the Creator, to man, the creature. As in the case of Sodom and Gomorrah, the result of this transference is that God will abandon such people to the most nefarious vices — lust of the flesh, lust of the eyes, lasciviousness and unmentionable sins.

When man and woman take God's honor for themselves, it is an unnatural act in the religious sphere and results in an unnaturalness in the moral sphere as well. Then the natural difference between man and woman, placed there by God at creation, is destroyed and both man and woman are stripped of their very nature as truly male and female. In an attempt to "modernize" and secularize God's Word people refuse to consider God and his revelation worthy of their acceptance. They do not like what they find in God's revelation and so they ignore or, perhaps even worse, change it to suit their own wishes.

For the pro-homosexuals, this means denying God's Word while self-righteously claiming they are true Christians. They revel with delight in sin without any pangs of conscience, because they have convinced themselves that God is only a God of love. They forget that he is also a just God, a "jealous God," a God who demands that his will be followed by his creatures. Because they forget or ignore God's will, we are told in Romans 1 that God "gives them over" to all kinds of sins.

In other inspired writing the Apostle Paul enumerates those sins: "I fear that there may be quarreling, jealousy, outbursts of anger, factions, slander, gossip, arrogance and disorder" (2 Corinthians 12:20). "The acts of the sinful nature are obvious:

sexual immorality, impurity and debauchery; idolatry and witchcraft; hatred, discord, jealousy, fits of rage, selfish ambition, dissensions, factions and envy; drunkenness, orgies, and the like" (Galatians 5:19-21). "We also know that law is made not for good men but for lawbreakers and rebels, the ungodly and sinful, the unholy and irreligious; for those who kill their fathers or mothers, for murderers, for adulterers and perverts, for slave traders and liars and perjurers — and for whatever else is contrary to the sound doctrine" (1 Timothy 1:9,10). "People will be lovers of themselves, lovers of money, boastful, proud, abusive, disobedient to their parents, ungrateful, unholy, without love, unforgiving, slanderous, without self-control, brutal, not lovers of the good, treacherous, rash, conceited, lovers of pleasure rather than lovers of God — having a form of godliness but denying its power" (2 Timothy 3:2-5). This "giving over" to sin was true in St. Paul's day and it is today.

Romans 1:26 is the only place in the Bible which speaks directly of homosexual females. It clearly states that the women abandoned the natural use of their female sexuality for an unnatural use. From what St. Paul says about the males in the same context (verse 27), it is obvious that with the women, too, homosexuality is meant. Therefore, female homosexuality or lesbianism is a violation of nature according to God's order.

In verse 26, the Greek words translated as "exchanged natural relations" depict a frightful exchanging, a horrible trading and perversion. This phrase brings out the enormity of violating even nature itself, established by God. The facts are plain and simple: People — male or female — desiring or engaging in sex with a member or members of the same sex abandon God's given natural order. This is contrary to his will.

There is absolutely no doubt as to the meaning of verses 26 and 27 concerning the sexual act. There is no word play in which the pro-homosexual writers can engage to change that meaning. But we shall see that they claim the reference is to heterosexual people rather than homosexual people! More on that later.

St. Paul speaks of one special vice — homosexuality — seen for centuries as the rudest, most perverse kind of lewdness. Even in secular society, certain taboos are commonly held. For example, incest and homosexuality are generally considered violations of nature. They mark the depth of immorality to which godlessness descends.

Sexual degradation always follows apostasy — the abandoning of the true faith. Sexual perversion and immorality run wild without God. The stench of sexual deviation is always evident when man rejects God's control over his life. It was that way in the days of Sodom and Gomorrah, in St. Paul's day, and today.

Look at Main Street America: massage parlors, adult bookstores, adult theaters, homosexual bars and baths, adult motels where you pay not by the night but by the hour, and pornographic magazines sandwiched between *Time* and *Good Housekeeping*. Besides that, most of the "adult" world is open twenty-four hours a day, seven days a week. Indeed, the sun never sets on America's smut. We are supposed to accept all of this as normal and natural.

No matter how loudly and long a person says he believes in God, if he willfully rejects God's will and continues to live in sin, then he is not really a Christian but an unbeliever.

In spite of this clear and plain portion of Scripture, Romans 1:26,27, pro-homosexual writers go through various linguistic gymnastics to twist and pervert God's Word. One such writer insists that this passage condemns only heterosexual persons actively committing homosexual acts. He wants the reader to believe that there is no condemnation of homosexuals or homosexual acts between homosexuals in this passage at all.

St. Paul is obviously not speaking of people who were forced into a singular homosexual act such as homosexual rape or even those who have experimented with homosexuality out of sinful curiosity and then abandoned it. The people St. Paul refers to in this passage were "given over" to shameful lusts. Natural relations were abandoned. They were inflamed with lust for one another, for people of their own sex. St. Paul describes a homosexual according to the pro-homosexual writers' own definitions. These people were by every inclination homosexual in regard to both men and women. To say that they could not be homosexuals because the "natural relations" for homosexuals is same-sex relations is begging the question. God recognizes only one type of behavior as natural. He did not create some people to be naturally heterosexual and others naturally homosexual. The natural relations are heterosexuality. This is made explicitly clear in verse 26 ("... women exchanged *natural* relations for *unnatural* ones") and in verse 27 ("... men also abandoned *natural relations with women* and were inflamed with lust for one another").

If one goes beyond or against God's intended order of creation, isn't that a sin? In Romans 1:26,27, the men and women are described engaging in sexual acts that are against nature — homosexuality. God has established the natural order of things and he demands that human beings stay perfectly within this natural order. This is his will. The practice of homosexuality does not allow a person to stay perfectly within this natural order.

ROMANS 1:18-32

The wrath of God is being revealed from heaven against all the godlessness and wickedness of men who suppress the truth by their wickedness, since what may be known about God is plain to them, because God made it plain to them. For since the creation of the world God's invisible qualities — his eternal power and divine nature — have been clearly seen, being understood from what has been made, so that men are without excuse.

For although they knew God, they neither glorified him as God nor gave thanks to him, but their thinking became futile and their foolish hearts were darkened. Although they claimed to be wise, they became fools and exchanged the glory of their immortal God for images made to look like mortal man and birds and animals and reptiles.

Therefore God gave them over in the sinful desires of their hearts to sexual impurity for the degrading of their bodies with one another. They exchanged the truth of God for a lie, and worshiped and served created things rather than the Creator — who is forever praised. Amen.

Because of this, God gave them over to shameful lusts. Even their women exchanged natural relations for unnatural ones. In the same way the men also abandoned natural relations with women and were inflamed with lust for one another. Men committed indecent acts with other men, and received in themselves the due penalty for their perversion.

Furthermore, since they did not think it worthwhile to retain the knowledge of God, he gave them over to a depraved mind, to do what ought not to be done. They have become filled with every kind of wickedness, evil, greed and depravity. They are full of envy, murder, strife, deceit and malice. They are gossips, slanderers, God-haters, insolent, arrogant and boastful; they invent ways of doing evil; they disobey their parents; they are senseless, faithless, heartless, ruthless. Athough they know God's righteous decree that those who do such things deserve death, they not only continue to do these very things but also approve of those who practice them.

An interesting point on this entire portion of Scripture is that every pro-homosexual writer whom I have read, reached the same conclusion concerning this passage. Yet each failed, in varying degrees, to make the proper application. The sins listed — lying, idolatry, lust, homosexuality, greed, depravity, murder, etc. — are results, not causes. The cause is explicitly detailed in verse 21, "For although they knew God, they neither glorified him as God nor gave thanks to him."

The cause comes from not worshiping the true and living God. When people no longer love God and try to live according to his divine will, all sorts of wickedness arise. God turns people over to the sin of homosexuality and all the other sins listed in this chapter. The cause and root of all sin lies in rejecting God as the only true and living God, and in failing to make him our number one priority as the First Commandment demands, "You shall have no other gods before me" (Exodus 20:3). This is evident in the very first sin of Adam and Eve. If we could keep the First Commandment, theoretically we could keep all the others.

The sins of homosexuality, false religion, gossip and boasting — the whole list — are symptoms of the condition of the old Adam within us when we are apart from our Savior, Jesus Christ. All of these sins stem from man's basic sin, failure to honor, obey and worship God as God. Therefore, the person who insists on practicing homosexuality (or any other sin) can not by definition be a Christian and worship the true God.

Nevertheless, advocates of homosexuality contend that true homosexuality is more than what is described in Romans 1:26,27. They say it is a state of being, a condition that is not chosen by people but is thrust upon them by society, physiology or even God. As believers, we know that because homosexuality is forbidden by Scripture, it cannot come from God. It may come from society; it may even be found to be a physiological or psychological disorder in some, perhaps akin to psychosomatic diseases such as some forms of colitis, asthma, migraine headaches, or even certain allergies. But regardless of the cause, it would still be the result of sin and remain a sin in God's eyes. It may be a person's cross to struggle with through life, just as an alcoholic bears the cross of never being able to take a drink. Like the homosexual, that person must strive, with God's help, to carry that cross without stumbling into the sin.

From our study of Romans 1, we see that homosexuality is one part of a bigger picture. It is one aspect of mankind's bondage to sin. Like other sins, homosexuality is the result of rejecting God and his plan for mankind. As man has drawn away from God, God has given him over to vile affections and vices.

Part of God's righteous judgment on the sin of idolatry — man not giving God first place in his life — is that God leaves man to his own self-damning devices, leaves him alone, and removes his grace. We dare not fault God for this either, because God grants us his grace. It is his gift to those that believe in and obey him. So the practicing, unrepentant homosexual is outside of God's grace, no matter how adamantly he or she insists otherwise. Such a person is in need of God's clear and unchanging law and his sweet and comforting gospel, reflected by us, his ambassadors.

4. Further New Testament Passages Speaking of Homosexuality

1 CORINTHIANS 6:9-11; 1 TIMOTHY 1:9-11

Do you not know that the wicked will not inherit the kingdom of God? Do not be deceived: Neither the sexually immoral nor idolaters nor adulterers nor male prostitutes nor *homosexual offenders* nor thieves nor the greedy nor drunkards nor slanderers nor swindlers will inherit the kingdom of God. And that is what some of you were. But you were washed, you were sanctified, you were justified in the name of the Lord Jesus Christ and by the Spirit of our God.

We also know that law is made not for good men but for lawbreakers and rebels, the ungodly and sinful, the unholy and irreligious; for those who kill their fathers or mothers, for murderers, for adulterers and *perverts*, for slave traders and liars and perjurers — and for whatever else is contrary to the sound doctrine that conforms to the glorious gospel of the blessed God, which he entrusted to me.

We shall consider these two passages together since they are very similar and the same Greek word for homosexual or homosexual behavior is used in both.

Before we discuss the two passages together, some comments on the word translated "male prostitutes" in 1 Corinthians 6:9 are in order. This same word (*malakoi*) is used in Matthew 11:8

("... what did you go out to see? A man dressed in fine clothes? No, those who wear fine clothes are in kings' palaces") and Luke 7:25 ("... what did you go out into the desert to see? A man dressed in fine clothes? No, those who wear expensive clothes and indulge in luxury are in palaces"). It means "soft, soft to the touch, delicate." When referring to human beings it came to mean a man or boy who allows himself to be used as an instrument of unnatural lust and is effeminate. The authoritative Greek dictionary, *Bauer-Arndt-Gingrich*, defines it this way: "of persons — soft, effeminate, especially of ... men and boys who allow themselves to be misused homosexually." This word was often applied to obviously homosexual persons in classical Greek literature.

It appears that this perfectly good Greek word had been distorted in much the same way that "gay," a perfectly good English word, has come to mean "homosexual" today. The non-Biblical writings of that day do strongly suggest that this word was used to refer to the passive partner in a homosexual relationship.

It would appear as though St. Paul in 1 Corinthians 6:9 is naming both the passive and active homosexual acts: "... male prostitutes ... homosexual offenders." Both roles are forbidden. (The active role refers to the male who performs fellatio or who penetrates in anal intercourse.)

The same Greek word (*arsenokoitai*) is translated as "homosexual offenders" in the 1 Corinthians passage and as "perverts" in the 1 Timothy passage. It is a compound word formed from the words for "male" and "marriage bed" and means something like "males who go to bed." In this sense, it would be the sexual partner who assumes the traditional active role. *Bauer-Arndt-Gingrich* defines it as a male homosexual, pederast, sodomite. The word is used in this sense in both secular and religious writings of the time.

St. Paul appears to have been the first or one of the first authors to use this word and it appeared only infrequently after him. Yet even if the word appeared only once in all of literature, there still would be no question as to its meaning. The authors of most dictionaries have always agreed with the Bible translators by giving the definition as "sodomite" or "homosexual."

The fact that Paul did not use one of the many words in Greek pro-homosexual literature to refer to sodomites or homosexuals probably means that he wished to leave no doubt as to the unacceptability of homosexual desire and behavior. He would not even legitimize homosexuality by referring to it in the same way its perpetrators did.

I have followed this same principle throughout this book and not referred to homosexuals in euphemistic terms like "gays," since that term somehow lessens the gravity of such sinful behavior. For the opposite reason it also explains the widespread use of the word "gay" among the homosexual community.

As you may have guessed, some pro-homosexual writers again resort to linguistic gymnastics in an effort to discount the translation of this Greek word as "homosexual offenders" and "perverts." Much is made of the fact that the famous Greek writer Plato, who often wrote of homosexual love between men, never used the word which St. Paul chose to use under divine inspiration by the Holy Spirit. But Plato also recognized that homosexuality was against nature, using the same phrase employed by St. Paul in Romans 1:27 (. . . abandoned natural relations. . .).

Other pro-homosexual writers insist that it is not homosexuality *per se* which is being condemned in these passages but only homosexual activity. They suggest that the word in question refers only to anal intercourse among men without offering any reasons why fellatio or other homosexual behavior is excluded. After trying to make that point, they then destroy their whole line of reasoning by saying that it is true, according to these passages, that this type of behavior (anal intercourse among men) excludes one from the kingdom of heaven. In other words, they are trying to make a distinction between the state of being a homosexual and homosexual behavior.

Even if the Apostle Paul were not speaking of homosexuality (although it is abundantly clear that he is), he is stating that the *behavior* of the homosexual (taking a member of one's own sex to the marriage bed, anal intercourse, fellatio, etc.) excludes a person from the kingdom of heaven. While this line of reasoning by pro-homosexual writers is intended to help the "Christian" homosexual, it obviously does not. After all, what's the use of being a homosexual if you can't do what a homosexual does? So repent, and trust in God's help to amend this sinful way of life.

Perhaps a few more remarks about each passage individually are in order. In 1 Corinthians 6:9-11 (". . . wicked . . . sexually immoral . . . idolaters . . . adulterers . . . male prostitutes . . . homosexual offenders . . .") St. Paul lists sins that were rampant when he came to Corinth. They were gross sins, humanly speaking. The only way to deal with such sinners is to prick their conscience with a harsh, stern word of the law: people that live in such sins shall not enter the kingdom of heaven. That word is clear and final. The people to whom St. Paul was writing knew God's law and knew that they had been set free from the bondage of sin by the gospel. But apparently, some were in danger of returning to that slavery, feeling that since their sins were forgiven anyway, they didn't need to worry about sin.

So St. Paul writes clearly. In an inspired effort to stem the rising tide of wickedness he pulls no punches. Paul wanted to make sure that his readers knew, in no uncertain terms, that the liberty given by acceptance of the gospel did not mean libertinism — the right to do whatever they pleased. God's grace does not give anyone the freedom to sin. So intent was St. Paul to be completely and unequivocally understood that he specifically listed fornicators, idolaters, adulterers, those addicted to sensuality and the homosexuals among those who flagrantly violate the holy will of God. God's people are *not* to be numbered among those who do such things.

In this passage, there is a very important message to homosexual and heterosexual people alike. The message is that *change is possible*, because of our Savior's victory over sin, death, and the devil. That victory is ours by faith. We need to remember to whom St. Paul was writing. He was writing to Christians. And what does Paul say to these Christians? He says that some had been the very sinners he had described in these verses. Imagine that! Fornicators, idolaters, adulterers and homosexuals! But they had been changed. By the power of the Holy Spirit working through the means of grace — the gospel in the Word and sacraments — they had come to know Jesus Christ as their Savior. They had consequently become new creatures as well, striving to drown their old Adam and sinful lusts each day.

This is true of all Christians for all times. We must remember Christ's promise and its fulfillment and live according to our new calling each day. St. Paul's inspired words are a message of hope to anyone with a propensity toward the sin of homosexuality. He tells us clearly that there was salvation for Christians who had formerly engaged in homosexuality but were no longer continuing that kind of life.

The vast majority of psychologists and therapists working with homosexuals today insist that for the most part, no change in the homosexual is necessary and that indeed change is not possible for the homosexual. This, quite simply, is a lie. Just as with any sin or temptation, for the Christian who must fight against the sin of homosexuality everyday the *possibility of change* is the very heart of the matter. Let there be no mistake about it, change is not easy. As we know from the Romans 1:26,27 passage ("Because of this, God *gave them over*"), homosexuality is a sin which can take over the life of the sinner. It is addictive and pervasive. Yet, with the help of God, there can be change.

The Christian who has been properly instructed in God's Word knows this. He is familiar with our Savior's statement in Mark 10:27, "With man this is impossible, but not with God; all things are possible with God." It is from God's Word that the Christian struggling against the sin of homosexuality will receive his inspiration and strength to overcome this treacherous vice. Just as with any other sin, his fellow Christians must be ready to apply the law and the gospel at the right time and in the proper amounts to assist him in his battle.

In the 1 Timothy 1:9-11 passage ("ungodly . . . unholy and irreligious; for those who kill their fathers or mothers, for murderers, for adulterers and perverts, for slave traders and liars and perjurers"), we see St. Paul listing sins, in order, against the Ten Commandments. We note that homosexuality is listed as a sin against the Sixth Commandment — the commandment against adultery. As violators of the Sixth Commandment, St. Paul mentions not only adulterers but sodomites. These are people who abuse their fellow men or women for the sake of gratifying their sexual lust in either a "natural" or an "unnatural" way. Both are sinful and both exclude the practitioners from the kingdom of heaven. But this is more than a simple condemnation of illicit sexual acts brought about by force against one party's will. Adultery doesn't have to be rape any more than illicit homosexual acts have to be rape. Adultery between or among consenting adults is wrong just as homosexual acts between or among consenting adults is wrong.

When looking at this 1 Timothy 1:9-11 passage, we should draw particular attention to the placement of the words. St. Paul mentions "sodomites" or "perverts" immediately after he speaks of "adulterers." He puts them in the same classification. While the reference here is *directly* to *male* homosexuals —sodomites (Genesis 19:5) and "abusers of themselves with men" (Romans 1:27 and 1 Corinthians 6:9) — it is an *indirect* reference to *all* homosexuals, male and female.

Luther shares a most interesting observation on this passage. He says that even the godlessness mentioned by St. Paul in the passage can serve the good of the Christian, and that it indeed *must* serve his good.

> After all, everything must redound to our good and produce benefits of various kinds. First, we thereby become accustomed to handle and hold the Word of God with greater diligence and so become increasingly certain of the truth. For if such factious sects, through which the devil wakes us up in this way, did not exist, we would become too lazy, would sleep and snore ourselves to death, and both faith and the Word would become obscured and would rust in our midst until actually everything would be ruined. But now these sects are our whetstones and polishers; they whet and grind our faith and doctrine so that, smooth and clean, they sparkle as a mirror. Moreover, we also learn to know the devil and his thoughts and become prepared to fight against him. All this would be lacking if the factious sects did not disturb us.[7]

So the next time some difficult problem or sin or worrisome situation confronts us, we can yet thank God because it forces us to dig deeper into his Word; to get down on our knees and implore his strength, guidance and wisdom; and to face the devil head-on. I have come to see the researching and writing of this book in that light.

As we leave these two passages, it should be obvious that the Holy Scriptures do indeed condemn the sin of homosexuality — homosexuality as it was in St. Paul's day and homosexuality as it is in our own time. Yet it is not a sin from which there is no escape. Thank God, through Christ's redemptive work and sacrifice, there is no such sin! May God's love, that caused him to send his one and only Son to be the Savior of the world, always be reflected by us as we deal with those trapped in homosexuality, recognizing that sometimes the strongest and greatest love is firm and hard and tough. In this connection, think of Christ's forgiveness and reinstatement of Peter recorded in John 21:15-19:

> When they had finished eating, Jesus said to Simon Peter, "Simon son of John, do you truly love me more than these?"
>
> "Yes, Lord," he said, "you know that I love you."
>
> Jesus said, "Feed my lambs."
>
> Again Jesus said, "Simon son of John, do you truly love me?"
>
> He answered, "Yes, Lord, you know that I love you."
>
> Jesus said, "Take care of my sheep."
>
> The third time he said to him, "Simon son of John, do you love me?"
>
> Peter was hurt because Jesus asked the third time, "Do you love me?" He said, "Lord, you know all things; you know that I love you."
>
> Jesus said, "Feed my sheep." . . . Then he said to him, "Follow me!"

Of course, an entirely different conclusion is drawn by pro-homosexual writers. They insist that we must pass judgment on St. Paul, this servant of the Lord and his inspired writings. They want us to see St. Paul as a wonderful interpreter of the gospel for his day. They suggest that his writings are still beneficial today but that his interpretations and applications of the gospel are fallible and out of date for us in the twentieth century. Certainly St. Paul was a sinner; he was the first to admit that in 1 Timothy 1:15 ("Christ Jesus came into the world to save sinners — of whom I am the worst"). But when he was privileged to write the inspired words of God, he wrote without error.

JUDE 7

> In a similar way, Sodom and Gomorrah and the surrounding towns gave themselves up to sexual immorality and perversion. They serve as an example of those who suffer the punishment of eternal fire.

The Greek words which are here translated "gave themselves up to . . . perversion" literally mean "going away after different or strange flesh." Among the Greek and Bible scholars there is varying opinion as to what that "different flesh" really was. Since it is used in reference to Sodom and Gomorrah and with the word which means to "commit fornication" the simplest explanation is that it refers to gross sexual sin, namely homosexuality. Other suggestions include adultery (someone who is not your spouse would be "different flesh") and bestiality.

Some have even suggested that Jude is here making reference to a Jewish legend which says that the *women* of Sodom had sexual intercourse with the angels who visited Lot disguised as men. One can almost understand how such a legend may have arisen. To the women of a city filled with homosexual men, two apparently heterosexual men must have seemed heaven-sent. The sitcom "Sarah," set in San Francisco, played a similar situation for laughs. Sarah's friend urged her to attend a party because they were flying in heterosexual men from the Midwest.

One of the first rules of interpreting the Bible is that the simplest interpretation is usually the best. That being the case, it can be interpreted that Jude 7 does indeed speak of and condemn homosexuality when taken in the light of the rest of Scripture. However, this passage should only be used to condemn homosexuality when it is used in connection with other clear passages of Scripture referring to this sin.

CONCLUSION

In conclusion, the Scriptures are very explicit in their condemnation of the sin of homosexuality. The person who lives in such sin is plainly excluded from the kingdom of heaven. It is also clear from 1 Corinthians 6:11 "once a homosexual, always a homosexual" is no more a truism than "once a drunk, always a drunk." There may always be a propensity for this particular sin. But, as with any sin, with the help of the Holy Spirit and fellow Christians, people may resist the temptation. Homosexuality, like most sins, is a sin which enslaves, but it is also, like all sins, a sin from which our Savior has freed us.

Unfortunately, homosexuality will continue to enslave and damn any who refuse to acknowledge it as sin or who are duped into believing that it is not a sin but a viable alternative by those claiming to be theologians and Bible scholars. Some of these pro-homosexual writers would even have us believe that the people of biblical times were completely unfamiliar with the terms and concepts of homosexuality. They remind us that modern psychologists and sociologists have given us the terms heterosexual and heterosexuality, bisexual and bisexuality, homosexual and homosexuality, and sexual orientation. They would have us believe that the ancient apostles and evangelists who wrote the Old and New Testaments had no concept of these things.

What they are saying, in effect, is that God's inspired Word is no longer applicable for our enlightened age. They ask us to pity the poor writers of the Bible who could only call a sin a sin instead of some fancy word that was concocted to give validity and respectability to man's basest desires and his rebellion against God's will. Just like the old saying "a rose is a rose is a rose," even the ancients knew what homosexuality was — regardless of the name given it.

At this point, perhaps a brief summary of the pro-homosexual writers' contentions regarding the biblical injunctions against the sin of homosexuality is in order. Most agree that the only place the Bible clearly prohibits homosexuality and homosexual relations is in Leviticus. They quickly dismiss this prohibition of homosexuality because it called for the death of those who practiced homosexuality. They insist that the death penalty is not in keeping with the ideals of the Christian community today and so must be dismissed as not applicable in our day and age. Secondly, these writers suggest that the account of Sodom and Gomorrah does not condemn the sin of homosexuality but poor manners in regard to hospitality. Thirdly, they try very hard to convince us that the New Testament passages speak only of heterosexual persons who engage in homosexual acts. This, they claim, is wrong because it is against the nature of a heterosexual. Since homosexual acts come naturally to homosexual persons, St. Paul and St. Jude were not condemning homosexuals. Finally, they insist that the passages we have studied in this chapter must be considered in the light of modern psychology, sociology and psychiatry, none of which are exact sciences.

Overall, what they ask us to believe is that *man's* will must be placed above *God's* will because it is not convenient or contemporary to accept the good and perfect will of the almighty and gracious Creator, Redeemer and Sanctifier.

There have been many books written which have tried to harmonize the sin of homosexuality with the Bible. Some are very well-written both in research and in style, even though they draw faulty conclusions. They have a tremendous appeal to the Christian who has a propensity for the sin of homosexuality; to the Christian parent who is trying to cope with a child who is caught in this sin; and to the parish pastor who wishes to pacify the members of his flock desiring to remain in this sin. Currently, the most popular of these books is *Christianity, Social Tolerance, and Homosexuality* by John Boswell. Boswell has written a "very big book." It has become nothing less than a watershed in the current thinking of many Christians on homosexuality. It undoubtedly has and will continue to do a great deal of damage and disservice to those Christians struggling with the sin of homosexuality.

God grant us the wisdom, the desire, the courage, and the strength to effectively counteract it and others like it! May he help us to stand with his Word in all its truth and purity.

5. SOCIETY SPEAKS OF HOMOSEXUALITY

GROWING ACCEPTANCE

No doubt homosexuality has been around since the earliest times. We have seen overwhelming evidence of its long time existence in chapters 2, 3 and 4 of this book. In modern day America and in other countries of the free world there seems to be an explosion of interest in the subject. People are being encouraged to "come out of the closet" and stop hiding their sexual preference. Others are being urged to accept homosexuals for what they supposedly are — ordinary human beings with a different sexual orientation. Housing and job discrimination against people because of their sexual preference is being outlawed as pro-homosexual lobbyists work hard on legislators.

Social tolerance of homosexuality is growing at a frightening pace. Homosexuality was once despised, punished, hidden and repressed by the individual, society and the law. Today it is promoted as an acceptable and normal alternative lifestyle. Young people with a propensity toward homosexuality are allowed and even encouraged by their parents, friends and peers. The various media and especially the entertainment industry, sports heroes and rock idols, psychologists and counselors add to that encouragement to follow one's inclinations. (We repeat here that people do *become* homosexual — they are not born that way!)

The entertainment industry has been a major contributor to the reshaping of America's views on homosexuality. Almost every month it seems that the television networks present at least one show dealing with the controversial issue of homosexuality. This is often a blatant attempt to appeal to the prurient interests of the viewers. The pay-television network Showtime even has a hit series called *Brothers* which centers around one of the brother's homosexuality. The Broadway show *La Cage Aux Folles*, which has a homosexual theme that glorifies transvestism, won six Tony awards in 1984. It has made a successful tour of the "conservative" Midwest where people are not expected to laugh at this kind of sin so readily. *The Times of Harvey Milk* is a documentary film which tells the story of San Francisco's first openly homosexual councilman who was murdered by fellow councilman Dan White. It was narrated by author/playwright Harvey Fierstein and was nominated for an Academy Award, being hailed as the finest in advocacy filmmaking.

Just as constant exposure to anything eventually desensitizes and numbs the senses, bombardment with pro-homosexual presentations will eventually dull the sharpness of our God-given consciences. We finally give up fighting for what is right and God-pleasing and look the other way as thousands are led down the path of unrighteousness to the gaping jaws of hell's gates. The Roper Organization recently conducted a poll for *U.S. News and World Report.* On the issue of homosexuality, 52 percent vetoed the idea of a homosexual president, a result heavily influenced by older respondents. Although 62 percent found homosexuality basically wrong, only 33 percent said they would vote for a law allowing the firing of homosexual school teachers. The telephone poll of more than 1,000 Americans over the age of eighteen was subject to a sampling error of plus or minus four percentage points.

Homosexuals are making tremendous inroads in the legislative and judicial branches of this country. For example, on March 26, 1985 the United States Supreme Court ruled that the State of Oklahoma could not fire homosexual school teachers or teachers who endorse homosexuality. The justification for the ruling was that firing a homosexual teacher would be a violation of that teacher's First Amendment rights. This ruling denies the people of Oklahoma the power to protect their children from the subtle and blatant, conscious and subconscious recruitment of homosexuals. Remember, homosexuals can not propagate themselves; nor is anyone born homosexual. Their numbers increase only through recruitment!

In November 1985 the Conference of Lesbian and Gay Elected and Appointed Officials and Prospective Candidates was held in West Hollywood, California. It was believed to be the first of its kind and its participants plan to make it an annual event. The conference ended with a pledge by the participants to fight for homosexual rights to adopt children and to obtain legal recognition for partners with whom homosexuals live.

There seems to be a well-orchestrated plan to promote the acceptability of homosexuality. One part of that plan appears to be the highly visible, militant and proud homosexuals themselves. They often stage demonstrations and parades reminiscent of the anti-Vietnam era of the 1960s. They march regularly on college campuses, at state capitals, in major cities, and at our nation's capital. They border on defiance in their demands for social acceptance. Recently it was reported that about 3,000 participants in the Ohio-Michigan Lesbian and Gay Pride Parade in Columbus, Ohio, chanted, "Hell no, we won't go!" when a bomb threat was announced. This report appeared on the front page of the Ohio State University student newspaper, *The Lantern*, accompanied by a large picture of two handsome young men locked in a passionate embrace.

Politically, homosexuals are also becoming a formidable force. A report by *U.S. News and World Report* in July 1984, listed homosexuals as the seventh largest group of voters in the U.S. with seventeen million potential voters. The report also noted that gays and lesbians had more electoral power than Hispanics, Jews and farmers combined. The recent 1984 elections saw many "advances" for the homosexual community that would never have occurred just ten or twenty years ago. For instance, even after he was censured by his colleagues for having a homosexual affair with a teenage congressional page,

Gerry Studds was reelected as a U.S. representative from the state of Massachusetts. Representative Studds won that election with 56 percent of the vote. Ted Weiss, a representative from New York, has been lobbying hard to spend more and more of our tax dollars to find a vaccine or pill which will allow homosexuals to have dozens of sexual encounters in a single night without bothering to scrub and gargle. Perhaps most alarming is the fact that Representative Weiss won reelection with an astounding 82 percent of the vote! Those are our tax dollars being used to promote homosexuality and to make it "safe" for America.

There is every indication that the pro-homosexual community is going to be working even harder and with greater success in future elections to bring into power legislators who are sympathetic to their sinful cause. It is conceivable that more and more people seeking election to public office will find it necessary to support homosexual causes in order to get elected — just as many politicians embraced abortion to win votes.

There's little question that advocates of homosexuality can be very adept propagandists. And a special target of their propaganda seems to be religion. Old Testament Judaism and New Testament Christianity have historically been major deterrents to the social acceptability of homosexuality. Pro-homosexual writers make much of the fact that many church bodies and religious organizations are changing their views (and trying to change God's Word) on the sinfulness of homosexuality. They often cite statistics which attempt to show that the church has finally entered the age of enlightenment concerning homosexuality. In 1982 and 1983, for example, G. Sidney Buchanan, an expert on constitutional law and a law professor at the University of Houston, conducted a survey of 950 faculty members in religion departments of U.S. colleges and counselors. These people were chosen at random from the *Directory of the American Association of Pastoral Counselors*. The results of this survey are used by pro-homosexual writers to show that even religion no longer condemns homosexuality. Following are some statistics from that survey:

— 91 percent believe that the government should not regulate sex between homosexuals.

— 50 percent believe that homosexual relations are not immoral.

— 75 percent think adultery is morally wrong, 16 percent do not consider it wrong and the remainder are undecided.

— 87 percent do not believe adultery should be a crime.

— 53 percent think the legal system should limit marriage to opposite sex couples.

— 71 percent would approve of a male homosexual teaching in an elementary school.

— 18 percent listed themselves as Roman Catholics, 15 percent were Methodists, 13 percent were Baptists and 12 percent were Presbyterians.

Those figures appeared under the title: "Most Religion Teachers Believe Homosexuality Is Okay," in a Columbus, Ohio newspaper for homosexuals.

REACTION TO RELIGIOUS OPPOSITION

Understandably, high praise is given by the pro-homosexual community to the religious leaders who support homosexuals. On the other hand, those who defend the true scriptural position receive the most caustic of treatments. While homosexuals plead for and even demand social tolerance for their lifestyle, very often they are themselves completely intolerant of any view which opposes their own. In keeping with that characteristic, many pro-homosexual writers engage in what can only be termed as "assassination journalism" when it comes to certain religious leaders who oppose their views.

The Reverend Jerry Falwell is often the victim of journalistic attacks by pro-homosexual writers since he is visible and vocal in his opposition to homosexuality. He is often referred to as "the Reverend" Jerry Falwell and as Jerry Flaw-well in pro-homosexual newspapers and magazines. While we may not agree with everything that the Reverend Falwell believes, teaches and does, he is identified with conservative religious thinking and represents fundamental religious beliefs to most of the American people today. Therefore an attack on him and his "moral majority" is often an attack on all those who teach that the Bible means what it says.

At a recent meeting of the Commonwealth Club in San Francisco, Shirley Temple Black, the club's president, accused the

Reverend Falwell of causing the American homosexual community a great deal of pain. Falwell declared that he did not mean to cause pain and that the homosexuals brought that pain on themselves. He asserted that no one is born a homosexual and that people *choose* to be homosexuals. He reminded the homosexuals gathered at the meeting that God loves them but does not like what they are doing. Their lifestyle is wrong in God's eyes. After reporting Falwell's remarks, a pro-homosexual journalist reminded his reading audience to rest assured that the Creator made them to function as the creature S/He made them. He insisted that a homosexual must function as a homosexual in order to fulfill his or her "God-given" nature. So much of the time pro-homosexual writers reject everything that the Bible says about homosexuality and castigate those who believe in a literal interpretation of the Bible. At the same time, it appears to be very important for them to believe that God condones what homosexuals are doing in their sinful lifestyle.

Another area receiving a good deal of attention in the religious homosexual community is the alleged "Homosexual Marriage Rite." This alleged homosexual marriage rite is being presented as proof that homosexuality was accepted by the Christian church in its earliest years and that therefore we must accept it today. The purported proof that some early Christian churches had homosexual marriage rites doesn't make those rites or homosexuality proper, correct or God-pleasing. The inventions of man do not change the immutable will of God. God has revealed, in no uncertain terms, that homosexuality is a sin and nothing man does can change that.

Nevertheless, the editors of *The Concord*, the newsletter of "Lutherans Concerned," a pro-homosexual organization, have become very excited about some research being done on these rites. They recently reported that Yale professor of history Dr. John Boswell, author of *Christianity, Social Tolerance and Homosexuality*, is doing extensive research on an alleged ancient Christian rite used for lesbian and male homosexual couples. Boswell contends that the rites were in use from perhaps the middle of the fifth century to the beginning of the thirteenth century. The rite is supposedly called "The Making of Brothers." In the rite, the couple dedicate their relationship with the language of unashamed faithfulness and honest love. It also refers repeatedly to St. Serge and St. Bacchus, two fourth century martyrs who were soldiers and supposedly homosexual lovers.

As we said before, the discovery of such a rite from church history does not mean it has God's blessing. Nor should it really surprise or upset us. The church has been, is, and always will be filled with sinful people who try to legitimize their sin by getting the church to sanction it. If the church violates God's Word by what it condones, then the church is wrong. Its actions cannot be used as the standard of what is right and what is wrong in God's world.

In the church of Martin Luther's day man's traditions and teachings had been placed on an equal and even higher level than the Scriptures themselves. The church needed to be reformed according to God's Word. Sinful man, inside or outside of the church, cannot presume to sit in judgment on the holy Word of almighty God. Man is not to pick and choose what he wants to believe and follow in God's Word. Nor is it up to man to decide what he wants to reject in God's Word in order to suit his own sinful nature. Yet this very thing has been done in the name of the Christian church since the first century!

When people within the Christian church begin to have such a high regard for man's traditions and such a low regard for the Word of God, it's time to climb up out of that mire of sin. In Romans 1 St. Paul gave a long list of reasons for God's wrath against mankind. With Paul, we pause here for a breath of fresh air and proclaim a *Te Deum Laudamus*, "the Creator — who is forever praised. Amen" (Romans 1:25).

6. CHRISTIAN CHURCHES
SPEAK OF HOMOSEXUALITY

For the most part, reports on the various churches listed here will be made without comment. Such comments on the positions or activities within the church bodies would tend to be repetitious since many of the churches hold similar positions.

A few general comments are in order. For one thing, few major church bodies have official policy statements condoning homosexuality. Actions do speak louder than words, though. Therefore we must examine the practices tolerated within the church body and not merely the official statements to determine the actual policy toward homosexuality. This is in accordance with the directives of God's Word. "Dear friends, do not believe every spirit, but test the spirits to see if they are from God, because many false prophets have gone out into the world" (1 John 4:1). Moreover, we must remember that Satan is working the hardest among the members of the Christian church. To divide and weaken the body of Christ here on earth — the church — over an issue like homosexuality would be a tremendous victory for the devil. As we examine the following church bodies with regard to homosexuality, you can determine for yourself if Satan is winning on the battlefield.

ANGLICAN CHURCH

Anglican scholar, Dr. W. Norman Pittenger of King's College, Cambridge University, says he sees no reason why churches should not ordain admitted homosexuals. He described biblical prohibitions against sexual acts between persons of the same sex as "red herrings," the use of which, he said, is an indication of "benighted ignorance."

AMERICAN BAPTIST

In 1984, the General Board of American Baptist Churches approved a policy statement accepting remarriage for divorced Christians under certain circumstances. The same policy statement gives guarded approval to homosexual unions.

UNITED CHURCH OF CHRIST

The UCC has been ordaining avowed homosexuals into the public ministry since 1973, with the ordination of the Rev. Tom Mauer in Minnesota and the Rev. William Johnson in California.

EPISCOPAL

Bishop Paul Moore, Jr., of the Episcopal diocese of New York, considers it no "great new thing" that he ordained a known homosexual woman a deacon on December 15, 1975. But on September 13, 1985, lay delegates of the Episcopal church defeated a measure that would have allowed ordination of homosexuals to the priesthood. This action killed the proposal even though bishops and other clergy had voted for it. The Episcopal homosexual organization is called "Integrity." There are active chapters of Integrity on most major university campuses.

LUTHERAN

According to the *Lutheran Cyclopedia* published in 1975, on the basis of Genesis 1:27,28; 2:21-24; and Romans 1:26,27, Christians oppose homosexual marriage.

Lutheran Church — Missouri Synod. As early as 1977, *The California and Nevada Lutheran*, official organ of the district and a supplement of *The Lutheran Witness*, the official magazine of the LC-MS, carried a letter from one of its pastors which stated, "Some of my friends are gay. They are my brothers and sisters in the church. . . . I exhort us to accept all people, regardless of sexual orientation, as God's creation and as partners in meaningful dialogue." However, a positional paper on homosexuality from the LC-MS states:

> Whether a person has only a homosexual inclination (propensity), or whether he actually practices it, it calls for an acknowledgment of the fact that homosexuality is sin and therefore requires repentance. . . . We must recognize the fact that when we are dealing with the sinful hearts of men, repentance, which is a radical change of heart and mind, can be brought about only by application of the Word of God.[8]

American Lutheran Church — This church body does have a fairly extensive statement on homosexuality. It will be interesting to see how this statement will be made to mesh with the Lutheran Church in America statement quoted later in this chapter when the two church bodies merge.

1. Persons who do not practice their homosexual erotic preference do not violate our understanding of Christian sexual behavior.

2. The church regards the practice of homosexual erotic behavior as contrary to God's intent for his children. It rejects the contention that homosexual behavior is simply another form of sex behavior equally valid with the dominant male/female pattern.

3. Genesis 18:16-19, Leviticus 18:22 and 20:13, Romans 1:24-32, 1 Corinthians 6:9,10, 1 Timothy 1:10 were reviewed. We remain open to the possibility of new biblical and theological insights.

4. We agree that homosexually-behaving persons need God's grace as does every human being. We all need to hear the Word, to receive the sacraments, to accept the forgiveness God offers, to experience the understanding and the fellowship of the community of Christ. We all need the power of the Holy Spirit for ethical living. So saying we nevertheless do not condone homosexual erotic behavior. Nor do we condone idolatry, pride, disrespect for parents,

murder, adultery, theft, libel, gossip or other sins known in our circles. The sacrifice God finds acceptable from each of us is a broken spirit, a broken and contrite heart and a new and right spirit within us (see Psalm 51).

5. Truth, mercy, and justice should impel members of the ALC to review their attitudes, words, and actions regarding homosexuals. Christians need to be more understanding and more sensitive to life as experienced by those who are homosexuals. They need to take leadership roles in changing public opinion, civil laws, and prevailing practices that deny justice and opportunity to any persons. We all need recognition and acceptance as human beings known to and loved by God.[9]

In his book, *The Ethics of Sex*, Helmut Thielicke insists that being homosexual is nothing to be proud of but finds certain narrow circumstances in which homosexual expression is no sin. This position was promoted by a study done by Professors Gaiser and Starassli of the ALC's Luther Seminary in St. Paul, Minnesota. That study was released by ALC President David Preus.

In regard to the position on homosexuality in the new Lutheran church being formed by the merger of the Lutheran Church in America, the American Lutheran Church, and the Association of Evangelical Lutheran Churches (a splinter group of the Lutheran Church — Missouri Synod), the book *Embodiment* sheds some light. It wants the new church body to allow unrepentant homosexuals as members, to recognize homosexual marriages and to have homosexual clergymen. The book is published by the ALC's Augsburg Publishing House and has been highly praised by ALC clergymen and professors.

In researching this book, I sent brief questionnaires to clergymen whose names I had received from The Ohio State University Gay Alliance. These clergymen have ministries to the homosexual community in the Columbus, Ohio area. I did not receive a reply from the Lutheran campus pastor who has such a ministry but I did receive one from a professor of pastoral theology at Trinity Lutheran Seminary in Columbus. This seminary is operated jointly by the ALC and LCA. My questions and his response follow:

1. Does the Bible teach that homosexuality is a sin?

ANSWER: It depends a great deal upon how you understand the concept of "sin"; in the Lutheran sense, *all* human behavior involves both sin and health; sexual behavior perhaps is more vulnerable because of the egocentric element involved in it. . . . Homosexuality perhaps is even more vulnerable.

2. How do you understand Romans 1:26,27?

ANSWER: Paul is here describing human behavior and identifying the simple consequences of that behavior: (if you eat too much you get fat, for example) if you "use" each other sexually, you pay certain consequences — God is the God of an "orderly" (consequential) universe. *Any sexual* obsession results in *idolatry*.

3. How do you understand 1 Corinthians 6:9?

ANSWER: Same as "you cannot serve two masters" (Jesus). Any obsession, sexual or otherwise, becomes a form of idolatry (worship) which ultimately rejects God. In another sense, any form of behavior which assumes ascendancy over faith/trust in God is sin . . . including homosexual behavior as well as heterosexual behavior.

4. What about promiscuity? Are homosexual couples required to be sexually faithful to one partner as heterosexual couples are? If not, Why?

ANSWER: Yes, the homosexual has the same responsibility that every other person has for the "appropriate management" of his/her sexuality.

5. If we believe human sexuality is a gift from God, then do you believe that heterosexuality and homosexuality are equal gifts from God?

ANSWER: They can well be. I do not believe they are the same since they serve different purposes in the economy of God. The *central* reason/function of sexuality in creation is the *bonding* ("one flesh") of two human beings. The secondary reason is procreation. Homosexuality may fulfill the first function, but cannot fulfill the second.

6. In your ministry, do you ever try to encourage a homosexual to practice heterosexuality in a God-pleasing way?

ANSWER: Yes.

7. How would you counsel a homosexual who is married to a heterosexual, or vice versa?

ANSWER: The same way I would counsel a heterosexual who is married and who is having an extramarital affair.

Lutheran Church in America — As mentioned earlier, this church body also has an official statement of homosexuality. It states:

Scientific research has not been able to provide conclusive evidence regarding the causes of homosexuality. Nevertheless, homosexuality is viewed biblically as a departure from the heterosexual structure of God's creation. Persons who engage in homosexual behavior are sinners only as are all other persons — alienated from God and neighbor. However, they are often the special and undeserving victims of prejudice and discrimination in law, law enforcement, cultural mores, and congregational life. In relation to this area of concern, the sexual behavior of freely consenting adults in private is not appropriate subject for legislation or police action. It is essential to see such persons as entitled to understanding and justice in church and community.

"Lutherans Concerned" is a group of Lutheran homosexuals and homosexual supporters that was formed in 1974. This organization currently has thirty-three chapters in North America. *The Concord* is its quarterly newsletter. Excerpts from two articles in the 1984 No. 4 issue will suffice to give the flavor of this publication and show how insidious homosexuality among Lutherans has become. The first article I share with you is entitled "Coming Out is a Spiritual Action."

Recently, a gay/lesbian educational foundation held a conference entitled "Coming Home." Attached, as a subtitle, was this message: "For each area we are not 'out' in life, we lose more and more of our self-esteem." Although that's a concept phrased in secular terms, it carries a Christian truth. Self-esteem, in Christ, is the awareness of our ultimate value before God. To accept the Good News of God's unconditional love is to be born again. For the lesbian or gay Christian, to come out is, at last, to accept oneself as an imperfect child of God who is unconditionally loved. . . . To come out is to face ourselves as we really are: The self that our loving God *already knows* "and from whom no secrets are hid." . . . Gays or lesbians could flee from God (Genesis 3:9,10); or they can awaken to the sweet sounds of the Gospel (Romans 5:1-11; cf. vv 6-8). . . . We have the invitation of the Scriptures both to encourage coming out (facing ourselves), and to shape our reborn lives with integrity. "Work out your own salvation with fear and trembling," advises Paul. "God is at work in you, both to will and to work for his good pleasure" (Philippians 2:12,13). . . . Gay and lesbian believers need to also struggle with a *spiritual action*: coming out *to* the Church, *in* the Gospel, for in that action, they finally can know and testify how God is at work in them, how they are finally at peace, and why they are finally able to walk in hope.

Note how quick homosexuals are to denounce and reject St. Paul's inspired condemnations of homosexual behavior but readily quote him when it's convenient in an effort to legitimize their sinful position. Obviously, they want it both ways. They want to pick and choose which parts of God's Word they will believe and practice, while ignoring the rest of the inspired record. But St. John warns us that "if anyone takes words away from this book of prophecy, God will take away from him his share in the tree of life and in the holy city, which are described in this book" (Revelation 22:19).

The second article from *The Concord* is entitled, "Seminary Survival Skills." It was written by an anonymous student at Luther Northwestern Seminary, St. Paul, Minnesota.

First, you need to know that no Lutheran Seminary will ordain practicing homosexuals (whatever "practicing" means). What you may not be aware of is that most Lutheran Seminaries don't have an official policy for dealing with gay students. At a recent student forum, the president of Luther Northwestern was confronted by a student on this issue, to which he replied, "It's a secret policy," noting that if he were to reveal it, he would be in trouble with the seminary board. The main reason the policy toward gays is a secret is that it is bad press for a seminary to have one in the first place; to a seminary's benefactors this isn't supposed to happen at all among those preparing for ministry. (Pure and simple, it's maintaining the laity's ignorance.) For this reason it's good to be aware of what position you're in when confronted by the faculty/administration (which rarely happens). You can be in a position to work *with* the seminary to save face — yours and theirs.

In connection with *The Concord*, I would also like to direct your attention to the appendixes of this book. Appendix 1 is a copy of a regular feature in *The Concord* called "World News" and gives information concerning the current affairs of the homosexual community. Appendix 2 gives information about the "Reconciled in Christ" program designed to welcome homosexuals into the Lutheran Church.

UNITED METHODIST

The Rev. Michael Collins, a founding leader of Affirmation, an organization for homosexual United Methodists, died in New York on October 15, 1984 at the age of thirty-six. He had suffered from AIDS for about a year. He was a former staff member of the United Methodist Board of Global Ministries.

On October 26, 1984 the Judicial Council of the United Methodist Church, the second largest Protestant denomination in the U.S.A., upheld a ban on the ordination of "self-avowed practicing homosexuals." But the future of homosexual clergy may still be up to individual bishops in the regional conferences. Some of these bishops have indicated they are not going to ask ordination candidates about their sexual orientation. Bishop Jesse DeWitt of the Wisconsin Conference and Superintendent Bernard Kassilke of Madison, Wisconsin, oppose ordination of openly homosexual ministers — not on theological grounds, they say, but because of difficulty in placing such ministers in "understanding" parishes.

PRESBYTERIAN

A United Presbyterian magazine states that they do not see persons as sinful simply because of a particular sexual orientation. Rather, they see homosexuality related to heterosexuality in the way that left-handedness is related to right-handedness, and therefore as morally neutral. Secondly, sin is expressed not in a particular sexual orientation, but in failure to love others and to express that love in kind acts. In this view, homosexuality is sinful only if one's own pleasure is sought, without considering the effect on others. In the same way, they say, heterosexuality can be sinful.

Presbyterians concerned about their denomination's acceptance of the homosexual lifestyle have formed an organization to promote biblical sexuality. We pray that it is not too little too late.

QUAKER

An official publication of this church body states that people should no more deplore homosexuality than left-handedness. (That sounds very much like the Presbyterian statement.) The publication asserts that homosexual affection can be as selfless as heterosexual affection. Therefore homosexuality is not morally worse than heterosexuality. From a speech by Dwight Spann Wilson to Friends for Lesbian and Gay Concerns (Quakers) in Philadelphia in February 1984, we share the following quote:

> If someone says to you, "I am God," you don't believe it. If somebody says to you, you are inferior because you are not like they are, why should you believe it? The Church is as the Church does. If the Church is not filled with love, it is not the Church. . . . If somebody calls himself or herself a Christian and they have no love, they're not a Christian. I know that for me my foundation is a rock . . . that foundation is the Spirit. Jesus always lived his life according to Psalm 103:6, "God always does what is right and is on the side of the oppressed." That is clear. Jesus said, "Suffer unto me those who are weary and oppressed and I will give you rest." That is the position that Jesus took; how can anyone who calls himself or herself a Christian take a lesser position?

Again we note the selective quoting of only supportive Scripture passages in a futile attempt to prove a point against which the whole of Scripture clearly speaks.

52

ROMAN CATHOLIC

As is often the case with this widely diverse body, many conflicting reports on official policy and practice are being received. "Dignity" is the Roman Catholic homosexual organization corresponding to "Lutherans Concerned." They, too, have active chapters on most major university campuses. Archbishop John L. May has participated in "Dignity" sponsored prayer meetings, much to the delight of the members since this gives a certain ecclesiastical legitimacy to their organization. Archbishop May has said that the Roman Catholic Church teaches that "homosexual orientation" is not morally wrong, but "homosexual activity," as in sexual intercourse, is. Obviously, that portion of his statement was not to their delight.

Robert Nugent, S.D.S., from the Sacred Congregation for Catholic Education stated that homosexuality is listed along with adultery, fornication and masturbation by the Roman Catholic Church as mortal sins. The church body does not consider homosexuality a condition but an act of conscious will. Homosexuality is also referred to as a disorder by the Roman Catholic Church.

However, homosexual Roman Catholic priests are apparently great in number and have more clout than many members of the laity have previously imagined. Evidently there is a well-organized homosexual network within the ranks of the clergy. Their influence is widespread and this makes the issue difficult for even the Vatican to handle expeditiously. From 1927 to 1956 the Roman Catholic Church had strict screening processes which prevented homosexuals from entering the clergy, with rare exceptions. Between 1956 and the present, thirty-eight known homosexuals have been ordained in the diocese of San Diego, California alone. No other statistics were available to the author.

UNITARIAN UNIVERSALIST ASSOCIATION

In 1980, the UUA, meeting in conference at Albuquerque, New Mexico, resolved to advocate the hiring of openly homosexual and bisexual persons for leadership positions in local congregations and within the denomination. In July 1984, the

1,300-delegate body of the UUA, meeting on the campus of the Ohio State University, endorsed religious celebrations of homosexual unions. The UUA, which numbers 175,000 members, is the first major denomination in North America to give official recognition to such rites.

The First Unitarian Universalist Church of Columbus, Ohio has an active ministry to the homosexual community. The pastor of that congregation was kind enough to return my questionnaire. I share with you his responses to my questions.

1. Does the Bible teach homosexuality is a sin?

ANSWER: I do not believe that the attitudes of 2,000-3,000 years ago can set the standards for today. Judging by the great number of biblical injunctions which are ignored, neither do most people, Christians included.

2. How do you understand Romans 1:26,27 and 1 Corinthians 6:9?

ANSWER: Both passages are quite specific. Why was Jesus silent? Paul seems to have had a number of sexual hang-ups which Jesus lacked and Jesus, after all, should be the better qualified to define sexual practices for Christianity.

3. What about promiscuity?

ANSWER: I believe the less said about faithfulness in marriages the better. I see many signs that heterosexual couples are less than faithful. Since marriage is not possible for gay couples the pressure to be faithful is less strong. There are signs that this is changing as gays are learning to be committed.

4. Do you believe that heterosexuality and homosexuality are equal gifts from God?

ANSWER: Most assuredly yes. Since homosexuality seems to be "given" its source must be the same as heterosexuality.

5. In your ministry, do you ever try to encourage a homosexual to practice heterosexuality in a God-pleasing way?

ANSWER: A very judgmental question. It also assumes that homosexuality is chosen. It is not, as many a person who has fought against it in him/herself could tell you.

6. How would you counsel a homosexual who is married to a heterosexual, or vice versa?

ANSWER: A very difficult issue, one I have had counseling experience in. The end is usually divorce since the gay partner may wish gay sex, which, of course, breaks the marriage vows. Some couples seem to manage in what is, I suppose, an open marriage. Open marriages among straights don't work so I don't see how they could for a mixed gay straight relationship.

7. In your congregation, do your heterosexual members accept your homosexual members?

ANSWER: Our gay members are accepted by the overwhelming majority of the members who know about them. Since one can't tell a gay at sight, many members are unaware that we have gay members — couples as well as singles. We would under no circumstances separate them from the church community. It is theirs too.

8. Any comments or suggestions?

ANSWER: Your task is a difficult one particularly since I suspect your mind is made up. Have you met any middle class, professional gay people? You might be surprised how far they are from the "flaming queens" of the stereotype. There are gay Lutherans obviously; I know one at least. Too bad you can't meet the gay members of your church, there must be some but they doubtless are fearful of "coming out" lest they be judged sinful and ousted from the church. I wish you well in your task. I hope you are approaching it with the love, the compassion that is Christianity at its best.

As a follow-up to this pastor's suggestion, I did meet with some middle class professional homosexuals who are members of his church. They were very eager to impress on me how much like heterosexuals they are, how much they love their Savior and how much they depend on him for their salvation. They were not interested in hearing anything I had to say concerning what the Bible teaches about their chosen sinful lifestyle. It was truly sad and frustrating to see such well-intentioned people blinded to the truth of God's Word by the devil, the world and their own sinful flesh. God have mercy and bring them to a knowledge of the truth!

UNIVERSAL FELLOWSHIP OF METROPOLITAN COMMUNITY CHURCHES

This is a new denomination started from scratch in 1968 by and for practicing homosexuals. In 1981, it had 150 congregations in eight countries with some 29,000 members. Because of its attractiveness to homosexuals and because many conventional churches find it difficult to minister to homosexuals, it is growing rapidly. Columbus, Ohio has a UFMCC congregation which meets each week at the Unitarian Universalist Association Church (see above). The Columbus UFMCC pastor describes herself this way: "I am black, I am lesbian, I am woman . . . and I choose to be Christian." She made this statement at an observance of the Athens, Ohio Gay Awareness Week. Athens, Ohio is a university town. She is also the mother of six children and an ordained minister in the Metropolitan Community Church of Columbus. She said she believes that Scripture can be interpreted any way a person prefers and that society often interprets it to discriminate.

She also responded to my questionnaire and invited me to attend her services. Here are her responses:

1. Does the Bible teach that homosexuality is a sin?
ANSWER: No.
2. How do you understand Romans 1:26,27 and 1 Corinthians 6:9?
ANSWER: Isaiah 56:1-8 (v 8, "The Sovereign Lord declares — he who gathers the exiles of Israel: 'I will gather still others to them besides those already gathered' ") and Acts 10:9-36 (v 15, "Do not call anything impure that God has made clean," vv 34,35, "I now realize how true it is that God does not show favoritism, but accepts men from every nation who fear him and do what is right.")
3. What about promiscuity?
ANSWER: Morality is a part of each person as interpreted or accepted by each one. If you mean do I require [couples to be sexually faithful], how would I go about *enforcing* that? If you mean by God, just as heterosexual couples — God's law and spirit of the law is the same.

4. Do you believe that heterosexuality and homosexuality are equal gifts from God?

ANSWER: As are all forms of sexuality a gift from God.

5. In your ministry, do you ever try to encourage a homosexual to practice heterosexuality in a God-pleasing way?

ANSWER: Only if the homosexual is not truly a homosexual and seeks counseling in that manner.

6. How would you counsel a homosexual who is married to a heterosexual, or vice versa?

ANSWER: Counsel them about what? Luke 10:26,27 " 'What is written in the Law?' he replied. 'How do you read it?' He answered: 'Love the Lord your God with all your heart and with all your soul and with all your strength and with all your mind' "; and, 'Love your neighbor as yourself.' " See also John 3:16,17.

7. In your congregation, do your heterosexual members accept your homosexual members? Do you hold separate services for the homosexual community to avoid possible tensions?

ANSWER: Each accepts the other. We hold no separate services for heterosexuals and homosexuals.

In conclusion, let me say that as Christians we should not be concerned why the Word of God is often seemingly without effect on so many so-called homosexual Christians. They do not have the true Word. They or others that they trust have distorted the Word beyond recognition and thus hampered its effectiveness.

7. Speaking of the Cause of Homosexuality

A MATTER OF CHOICE?

Of necessity, this chapter is rather short. The Christian sees only one cause for homosexuality — sin. It is a sin against nature, society and, most of all, God.

By this time it should be abundantly clear to anyone who accepts all of the Bible as the inspired and inerrant Word of God that homosexuality is a sin. Since the fall into sin, we have all been born with original sin. As the Psalmist David declared, "Surely I have been a sinner from birth, sinful from the time my mother conceived me" (Psalm 51:5). Sin is a part of our old Adam which we carry with us as long as we live on this earth. For this reason, explains the Bible, we shall be burdened with sin and fighting against sin as long as we live in this world. Jesus says, "For out of the heart come evil thoughts, murder, adultery, sexual immorality, theft, false testimony, slander" (Matthew 15:19). No advocate of homosexuality whom I have read or with whom I have spoken would deny that the actions our Savior lists in Matthew 15:19 are sins. Nor do they deny that a Christian should not willfully live in such sin.

The advocates of homosexuality see homosexuality in an entirely different light. They insist that homosexuality or homosexual orientation is not a matter of choice but a fact of life.

Homosexual advocates maintain that it is not a conscious decision on the part of individuals, but a condition thrust upon people whether they wish to be homosexual or not. Proponents of homosexuality seem to take this theory as a foregone conclusion. They shake an accusing finger at anyone who would be so cruel and unloving and unchristian as to condemn homosexuality when God himself made some of his people that way. Ignoring or twisting the meaning of the scriptural injunctions against homosexuality, these misguided souls turn to the scientific and medical world for proof that they must be right and the Bible must be wrong. And so they fall into the trap of placing man's reason over God's Word. This has been the source of almost every heresy in the Christian church throughout the ages.

But what about that scientific proof of which they are so sure and proud? In spite of all the millions of governmental tax dollars and foundational grants spent on research in this area, there is little agreement on the cause of homosexuality. No scientific study of which I am aware has been able to make a solid and conclusive statement on the cause of homosexuality. No one can say with any degree of scientific certainty that any medical study has conclusively proved that homosexuality is caused by an abnormality in the genes, a glandular condition or hormonal imbalance. The reason researchers cannot determine a scientifically valid cause for homosexuality is, of course, because they are looking in the wrong places.

Homosexuality is not a medical problem. Nor is it, in and of itself, a psychological one. Homosexuality is, quite simply, a sin coming from the devil, the world and our own sinful flesh. The homosexual lifestyle is spiritual hypocrisy, for it violates nature and God's clearly stated law.

Many practicing homosexuals wil try to rationalize by telling you that to try to live a heterosexual life for them is a lie and against the nature God gave them. But such rationalization is a lie against God's Word. Since homosexuality is a lie, then we know from where it comes — the devil. Our Savior said of those who lie that they belong to the devil. "You belong to your father, the devil and you want to carry out your father's will. . . . When he lies, he speaks his native language, for he is a liar and the father of lies" (John 8:44). This simple explanation of homosexuality — that it is a sin — is mocked by the medical, scientific and homosexual communities in general.

One of the favorite statements of homosexuals is, "God made me this way." They are, I'm sure, thoroughly convinced that *they* had no choice in the matter whatsoever. What they do is not *their* fault and, therefore, society *must* accept them. Yet, as Jesus said, sin does not come from God but from within the sinner himself. "For from within, out of men's hearts, come evil thoughts, sexual lewdness, envy, slander, arrogance and folly. All these evils come from inside and make a man 'unclean' " (Mark 7:21-23). It is almost as if St. James were speaking directly, face to face, with modern advocates of homosexuality, when he wrote, "When tempted, no one should say, 'God is tempting me.' . . . each one is tempted when, by his own evil desire, he is dragged away and enticed," (James 1:13,14).

Some people are tempted by the sin of homosexuality; others are not. Those who are not can thank God for that blessing, but should not consider themselves better than those who are tempted by homosexuality. Undoubtedly, people who are not tempted by homosexuality are tempted by sins which may not bother others. Remember that Satan is very adept at tempting each of us to indulge in our own "pet" sins. St. Paul warns each one of us not to become proud and puffed up just because we may not have to battle a particular sin the way another person does. "Do not think of yourself more highly than you ought, but rather think of yourself with sober judgment, in accordance with the measure of faith God has given you" (Romans 12:3).

A SIN AGAINST NATURE, SOCIETY AND GOD

The person who is tempted by the sin of homosexuality must recognize the fact that it is a sin. He or she needs to see that it is a sin even against nature itself. God created human beings as male and female to complement each other, as we see in Genesis 1:27,28. "So God created man in his own image, in the image of God he created him; male and female he created them. God blessed them and said to them, 'Be fruitful and increase in number; fill the earth and subdue it. . . .' " When man needed a suitable helper, God did not create another man but a woman, taking her from man, to show the close bond between man and woman. "The man said, 'This is now bone of my bones and flesh of my flesh; she shall be called woman for she was taken out of man' " (Genesis 2:23). Even the physical makeup of the male and female body shows God's intention — they go together, they fit each other in a natural way that simply does not exist for the homosexual. Besides, God made people with a natural desire for the opposite sex: "For this reason a man will leave his father and mother and be united to his wife, and they will become one flesh," (Genesis 2:24).

Advocates of homosexuality continually insist that God does not say homosexuality is wrong (even though he clearly does). But for the sake of argument, we might ask them, where does God ever say that homosexuality is right? If it is supposed to be "the nature" of fully one-tenth of the crown of God's creation, the human being, it certainly seems he would have made it known that such desire and behavior meets with his approval. But it doesn't. Homosexuality is a sin against nature.

Homosexuality is also a sin against society. As we have said before, in most cases homosexuals choose not to propagate themselves and most children of homosexuals do not turn to homosexuality themselves. The sin of homosexuality is not, in that sense, genetic. Perhaps homosexual parents and the children of homosexuals can see better than others that the homosexual lifestyle is not natural and is wrong. Maybe the homosexual parents want a better life for their own children than the one they have chosen for themselves. Could it be that such parents want to spare their children the pain, guilt, frustrations, "one-night stands" and loneliness of the typical homosexual lifestyle? Is that why so few children of homosexuals turn to homosexuality themselves?

Yet, there is a conscious effort to increase the size of the homosexual community by encouraging people who may be fighting their sinful weakness toward homosexuality to drop their defenses and "come out." By "advertising" themselves as "normal," happy, healthy people they seek to convince others that it is perfectly normal to be one of them. Enticement into their way of life is the only way that the homosexual community can maintain and perpetuate itself. If society permits the acceptance of homosexuality to permeate the media and our schools (just try to find a major secular university or college without an active homosexual organization) then society will pay the price for its leniency and indulgence. Throughout history, the price has been the decline and destruction of that society.

Finally, homosexuality, like all iniquity, is a sin against God. Chapters 2, 3 and 4 of this book are proof of that. The necessity of twisting God's Word in order to make homosexuality appear acceptable is evidence enough that God does not view homosexuality as a viable alternative to his plan. The Lord does not bless homosexuality as an alternate lifestyle to the one he established at creation. Homosexuality is simply part of the diabolical scheme Satan has devised to ruin the crown of God's creation — human beings. Homosexuality is a sin against the body he has given us. God gives us a clear and special warning against such sexual sins. "Flee from sexual immorality. All other sins a man commits are outside his body, but he who sins sexually sins against his own body. Do you not know that your body is a temple of the Holy Spirit, who is in you, whom you received from God?" (1 Corinthians 6:18,19)

Since homosexuality is a sin against nature, society and God, it has only one ultimate cause — the devil. Those who practice homosexuality, reject God's grace of freedom from sin through Christ and belong to the devil. That is not a hate-filled statement aimed at homosexuals, but one filled with love for their souls and their eternal welfare.

8. SPEAKING OF THE CURE FOR HOMOSEXUALITY

CHANGE IS POSSIBLE

Mention a cure for homosexuality to one of its advocates and the reaction can verge on violent. This should not surprise us. It is not all that unusual in other areas of sin. Our own reaction is often similar when we realize that we must not indulge in our own pet sin, whatever that may be.

Our old Adam, that is, our sinful nature, constantly rebels against God's will. It is always looking for ways in which sin can continue to raise its ugly head in our lives. We have the most difficulty controlling our sinful urges when we are tempted by our pet sin. Therefore, we can expect that someone who is caught in the sin of homosexuality will vehemently defend his or her right to practice that sin. But no matter what defense is offered for this lifestyle, homosexuality remains a sin against God.

Since homosexuality is a sin, the Christian, out of love and thankfulness for all that God has done for him or her, will seek to avoid it. The person who has been practicing homosexuality and also wants to live a God-pleasing life must change his or her lifestyle so that it no longer includes homosexuality. By the grace of God and through the power of the Holy Spirit change for the homosexual *is* possible. But that change is often difficult because of the pervasive and consuming nature of the sin.

Another factor which makes change difficult is the propaganda offered by the homosexual community, some church bodies and much of society. They maintain that there is no need for the homosexual to change. Pro-homosexual writers insist that homosexuality is natural and that it even causes fewer problems in society than heterosexuality. For this reason, they suggest that the homosexual lifestyle should be emulated and seen as desirable. After all, they insist, homosexual relationships bring about no legal difficulties (although there is a "palimony" suit against the Rock Hudson estate pending); usually do not produce property-settlement difficulties; leave no spouses defenseless or unprovided for; and create no unwanted pregnancies or illegitimate offspring. Of course, the pro-homosexual writers choose not to mention the fact that sexual relations among promiscuous homosexual males do present the as yet incurable and always fatal disease called AIDS — Acquired Immune Deficiency Syndrome.

Most proponents of homosexuality see no need for the homosexual to change. Rather, everyone else, including the church, must change to meet the needs of the homosexual. They insist that on the basis of Christian love, people today must realize that a number of intimate relationships are possible for the individual. Since God is love and we are to love all people, they agree that it should not matter whom we love, intellectually or physically. They suggest that it is the responsibility of the church, its leaders and members, to lead the way in changing society's traditional attitudes toward sexuality and human relationships of all kinds. They want the Christian church to lead the way for the acceptance of homosexuality. But this kind of attitude skirts the issue and denies the problem. It will do the homosexual no eternal good to deny the sinfulness of his or her desire and behavior. Such a denial will lead only to eternal ruin.

Still, some homosexuals claim that the only way they can be happy here on earth is to give in to their homosexual desires and practice homosexual behavior. I do not believe that is the only way they can be happy or content. Even if it were, better to be unhappy here for fifty, sixty or seventy years than to suffer eternally in the fires of hell. Besides, the Christian's life is often pictured as a constant war which is why we are to put on the full armor of God. St. Paul encourages us, "Put on the full armor of God so that you can take your stand against the devil's schemes" (Ephesians 6:11). We are constantly at war with Satan, the world and our sinful flesh. And war is certainly not pleasant or happy. The continual struggle going on inside each Christian between the old Adam and the new man often causes us pain and frustration. Nevertheless, we can rejoice and be at peace at the same time. For we know that our Savior Christ Jesus has won the war for us. When we deny our sinfulness, we reject all that God has done for us. Then we must face the judgment of God without the robe of Christ's righteousness wrapped around us. The only result must be to suffer eternal damnation in hell.

After admitting the sinfulness of homosexuality the only way in which to overcome it is with Christ's love. There is no sin or bondage to sin which our Savior cannot break. He shed his blood on the cross of Calvary for all people, including homosexuals. John 3:16 is the only answer for a person caught in the sin of homosexuality: "For God so loved the world that he gave his one and only Son, that whoever believes in him shall not perish but have eternal life." Just as a murderer cannot become a child of God and continue killing or a thief be converted to Christianity and continue stealing, neither can a homosexual have true faith in his or her Savior and persist in homosexual behavior. "Jesus declared, 'Go now and leave your life of sin' " (John 8:11).

It is a sad fact of history that the Christian church has not always been as ready to give of Christ's love to the homosexual as the Bible instructs. Without treating sin lightly or taking it for granted, we must also extend the helping hand of Christ's love to all who are in need. To be sure, we must convince the individual of his or her sinfulness with the law, but we must also be ready to assure the repentant person of God's forgiveness. We need to follow the example of our Savior when he dealt with an adulterous woman (John 8:1-11). First he told the woman that he did not condemn her, then he told her to leave her life of sin. He showed love for her by saving her from execution. Out of love and thankfulness for her salvation through Christ, the adulterous woman was to leave her life of sin. First came Christ's love and salvation (which did not condone her sinful lifestyle), then came Christ's command to change. So often churches and Christians do the opposite. They tell the homosexual or others caught in "public" sins to change and then they'll love them. This is one area where the church does need to change with regard to the sin of homosexuality. We Christians need to be ready to help anyone fighting the temptations of sin — homosexual or otherwise. If that person is troubled by homosexuality, then we should be eager to encourage the struggle against it, to rejoice at the triumphs over it, and to help pick up the person after a fall into that sin.

Jesus Christ has given us an example to follow. Here we think of our Savior's parable of the prodigal son (Luke 15:11-32). This son offended his father, fell deeply into sin and almost despaired. When he repented of his sin and returned to his father, he was welcomed with open arms. His father even killed the "fatted calf" in order to celebrate in the best possible way. We think also of Simon Peter who was lovingly reinstated to discipleship after his sin of denial of our Savior (John 21:15-19). We need to love the person struggling against homosexuality with Christ's love — a love that never condones sin but is always ready to extend a Christian helping hand in the fight against it. We must never turn away from that person because of fear or revulsion.

Many churches and Christians are reaching out with the powerful love of Christ. Some go too far and "hallow" the sin of homosexuality, thus making the fate of the sinner worse than before. In an attempt to be "contemporary," instead of undertaking the more difficult task of helping the homosexual, many churches today choose the easier road of defending and excusing homosexual actions among Christians. Such churches cannot possibly offer the homosexual the help he or she so desperately needs. By ignoring God's judgment of the sin of homosexuality, they also take away Christ's grace which is necessary to overcome that sin.

So enslaving is the sin of homosexuality that a permanent "cure" may not be possible. That is, it may never be possible for a homosexual to have a life free from homosexual temptation. But it is not impossible for a homosexual to change. It is not impossible for a homosexual to resist that temptation. Speaking of salvation, our Savior said, "With man this is impossible, but not with God; all things are possible with God" (Mark 10:27). Change does not come easy for sinful man. Only through the power of the Holy Spirit, working through the means of grace (the gospel in the Word and the sacraments), can any person change his sinful life.

Some people in the medical community agree that change for the homosexual is possible, but difficult. Dr. Donald Tweedle, a clinical psychologist in suburban Los Angeles, doesn't believe that a "cure" necessarily implies a life free from homosexual temptation. He explains that many of his homosexual clients have gone on to live satisfactory heterosexual married lives. He views homosexuality in much the same way as alcoholism, classifying it as an addictive practice. Dr. Tweedle has counseled about three hundred homosexuals in twenty-five years of practice.

Like the recovering alcoholic, with God's help and the help of fellow Christians reflecting Christ's love, the homosexual can lead a life that gives glory to God by daily resisting the sin of homosexuality. It will be a joyful life according to the new man created in him or her by the Holy Spirit, even though the old Adam may hate and rebel against the God-pleasing way of life.

RESPONSES TO HOMOSEXUALITY

In conclusion, we can see three basic responses to homosexuality within the Christian church. The first and correct approach sees the Bible as God's totally inspired and inerrant Word, the only guide for our faith and life. With this approach, it is necessary to view homosexuality in the perspective of a scriptural understanding of sex. In God's creative design the two sexes are intended to complete and complement one another. In the beginning, to offset Adam's lack of human companionship, God fashioned not another man but a woman.

In support of God's plan of the lifelong marriage partnership of a man and a woman Jesus cites the Genesis record: "At the beginning the Creator 'made them male and female,' and said, 'For this reason a man will leave his father and mother and be united to his wife, and the two will become one flesh' . . ." (Matthew 19:4-6). *Nowhere* does the Bible say that two men or two women can achieve the same type of partnership of a man and wife in a God-pleasing way. Homosexual behavior is contrary to God's creation. It is contrary to his will for man's life as Romans 1:26,27 and 1 Corinthians 6:9-11 make plain (see chapter 5).

The second approach or response is the one which sees homosexuality as a sin according to God's Word, but instead of rejecting homosexuality as a proper way of life for the Christian, rejects the Bible instead. There are pro-homosexual writers who consider themselves Christians, know what the Bible says concerning homosexuality, and still advocate the right of the Christian to practice this sin. They freely admit that homosexuality is a sin according to the Bible. In the fact of that awareness, they insist on the homosexual's right to follow his inclinations. While this is certainly a sinful and dangerous position because it attacks God's Word, it is more blatant and more easily recognized as being wrong by most Christians than is the third approach to homosexuality.

The third approach to homosexuality in the Christian church is the most dangerous. It undermines saving faith in a more subtle way than the more open second approach. It is the approach which attempts to harmonize homosexuality with Scripture, using "theological jargon" to condone homosexuality. When such heresy is espoused by religious leaders and received by an uninformed Christian laity or a Christian with a propensity toward the sin of homosexuality, the result can be at first confusion, then tolerance and finally embracement.

This is a treacherous approach to homosexuality and to the Scriptures. To the enlightened Christian it is frightening how skillfully pro-homosexual writers can couch heresy within orthodoxy! They agree that Scriptures portray the primary will of God as being heterosexual attraction leading to a permanent marriage in which there is sexual fidelity. They state very clearly that this is the norm; that this is what is expected. But, they quickly point out exceptions to this rule. Pro-homosexual writers cite Jesus, Paul and others as examples of individuals who remained unmarried in response to the call of God so that they might more effectively carry out their particular mission in this world. After noting those exemplary (and we might add extraordinary) examples they remind us that the primary will of God may not be possible for all people because of certain conditions or situations.

We would agree that not all people have the opportunity to marry and some married people may not be able to fulfill the ordinary obligations of marriage due to illness or accident. Such conditions do not release them from the will of God. People are not free to seek and use other sexual outlets that are contrary to the expressed will of God. In opposition to this, the pro-homosexual writers suggest that a person in such a situation must seek out what God's will is for him or her at *this* time and not be too concerned about what God's Word has to say about conditions two to six thousand years ago. They want to make it possible for a person to rationalize away the fact that he or she is sinning; they argue that sometimes people's only option is to practice their homosexuality. This faulty logic leaves the door wide open for homosexuality, and the pro-homosexual writers make it sound as though God himself opened the door. Obviously, this is extremely attractive to the old Adam of a Christian who must fight against the sin of homosexuality.

Some pro-homosexual writers further muddy the clear waters of Scripture by condemning some forms of homosexuality while condoning others. They suggest that there are practices within homosexuality that are displeasing to God. They list coercive and exploitative homosexual sex, selfish, self-fulfilling homosexual sex and homosexual sex that disregards the worship of God among those practices which the Bible rightly condemns. That sounds pretty good. Then they go on to insist that when persons are homosexual — this being a persistent condition of sexual preference — and in love with each other, the rules of God's Word all of a sudden change. Supposedly, if two homosexual people love each other, are committed to one another, and want to have sexual relations with one another, then the biblical injunctions against homosexuality no longer apply.

Pro-homosexual writers even go so far as to suggest that such persons should also be allowed to serve God in the public ministry. This approach is so very dangerous because it subtly gives credence to the big lie in much the same way as those who insist "once a drunk, always a drunk."

In light of all this, we must preach and teach firmly against homosexuality as it becomes more and more accepted by this sinful world. There must be no doubt whatsoever concerning the sinfulness of homosexuality in the minds of Christians. The false climate of respectability created for homosexuality within society and the church is the very last thing a young person with a predisposition toward homosexuality needs. He or she must be encouraged to fight the good fight of faith.

We must do all we can to help in that fight, encouraging that young person in whatever way possible not to experiment with homosexuality, but to save himself or herself for heterosexual marriage. Nor can we self-righteously turn our backs on those men and women, boys and girls who are struggling against the sin of homosexuality, no matter how repulsive that sin may seem to us personally. We must also be ready and willing to counsel and aid the Christian struggling against the sin of homosexuality. This means that we must be approachable by anyone seeking our help. Only God knows how many of his children have had to shoulder a tremendous burden of guilt without the assistance of a fellow Christian, simply because they feared being ostracized by those who could help them the most. God help us all to follow the example of our loving Savior who ate with publicans and sinners, opened his arms to all, and forgave all kinds of sins!

9. SPEAKING OF AIDS

ACQUIRED IMMUNE DEFICIENCY SYNDROME

In homosexual communities across our country, everyone knows someone who has died of Acquired Immune Deficiency Syndrome (AIDS), someone who is dying of AIDS or someone who is simply scared to death of AIDS. The homosexual community has mobilized to fight AIDS. They have set up agencies to deal with the dying victims, lobbied public officials for more research money and tried to quiet public fear. As more of their friends and lovers are diagnosed and die every day, many homosexual men have changed the way they live. They are leaving the fast track of multiple anonymous sexual partners night after night for a middle ground with less chance of infection. Their efforts to care for the living dead and their worried friends are being highly publicized by the media to gain the sympathy of the heterosexual community. Sadly, some homosexual men continue to behave as if they were out of the disease's reach.

The heterosexual community is reacting to the AIDS epidemic with understandable though sometimes unreasonable fear. Fear of giving blood, of eating in restaurants where homosexuals may prepare and serve the food or even just wash the dishes, of using public restrooms, of treating AIDS victims or even attending school with a hemophiliac AIDS victim has become commonplace.

An abundance of misinformation has led to a near panic in some areas of the country. The purpose of this chapter is to give correct information on AIDS as we know it today, as well as a Christian perspective. The statistics and the facts from the ongoing research change almost daily. We shall endeavor to give the best information available at the present time.

Acquired Immune Deficiency Syndrome, or AIDS, was first reported in the U.S. in 1981. Since that time, the Public Health Service has received reports of more than 14,500 cases. About 50 percent of those cases have already resulted in death.

AIDS is a serious illness which has been named the number one priority by the U.S. Public Health Service. Researchers have been working for five years to identify the causes of AIDS and develop treatments and preventive measures.

AIDS does not actually kill its victims. Rather, AIDS makes the body vulnerable to serious illnesses which are not a threat to anyone whose immune system is functioning normally. These illnesses are referred to as "opportunistic" infections or diseases.

A virus causes AIDS. It has been given different names such as human T-lymphotropic virus, type III (HTLV—III); lymphadenopathy associated virus (LAV); or AIDS related virus (ARV). Infection with this virus does not always lead to AIDS. Most infected persons remain in good health; others may develop illnesses varying in severity from mild to extremely serious. At this time, it is generally accepted that anyone who develops AIDS will die within two years of diagnosis.

Most individuals infected with the virus have no symptoms and feel well. Those who develop AIDS have preliminary symptoms which include tiredness, fever, loss of appetite and weight, diarrhea, night sweats and swollen glands (lymph nodes) — usually in the neck, armpits or groin. Anyone experiencing these symptoms for more than two weeks should see a doctor.

Ninety-four percent of the AIDS cases have occurred in the following groups of people:

> 73 percent: sexually active homosexual and bisexual men with multiple partners.

17 percent: present or past abusers of intravenous drugs.
2 percent: persons who have had transfusions with blood or blood products.
1 percent: persons with hemophilia or other coagulation disorders.
1 percent: heterosexual sexual contacts of someone with AIDS or at risk for AIDS.

The remaining 6 percent of AIDS patients do not fall into any of these categories, but most researchers believe that transmission of the disease occurred in similar ways. Infants and children who have AIDS may have been exposed to the virus before or during birth.

Of the cases of AIDS in the U.S. 36 percent come from New York and 23 percent from California. Florida is third in the highest number of reported cases. So far, AIDS has occurred in forty-six states, the District of Columbia, Puerto Rico and more than thirty-five other countries.

In spite of all this, AIDS is *not* a highly contagious disease. AIDS is difficult to catch, even among people at highest risk for the disease. No cases have been found where AIDS was transmitted by casual household contact. The AIDS virus has been found in saliva and tears but there have been no cases reported from exposure to either. Ambulance drivers, police, firefighters, doctors, nurses and health care personnel have not developed AIDS from helping or caring for AIDS victims. The risk of catching or transmitting AIDS from daily contact at work, school or at home apparently is statistically nonexistent. Of course, anyone who comes in contact with AIDS victims should carefully follow common sense safety and hygiene procedures as with any potentially transmissible diseases.

AIDS is spread in three ways: sexual contact, needle sharing or, less commonly, through blood and its components. It may be transmitted from an infected mother to an infant before, during or shortly after birth. The risk of getting AIDS is greatly increased by having multiple sexual partners, either homosexual or heterosexual. The sharing of needles among those using illicit drugs can result in the transmission of the AIDS virus. The innocent victims of AIDS are the hemophiliacs and persons receiving blood transfusions.

The incubation period for AIDS (the time between infection with the virus and the development of symptoms) seems to range from about six months to five years and possibly longer. But remember, not everyone exposed to the virus develops AIDS.

At the time of this writing there is no single test for diagnosing AIDS. HTLV—III antibodies can be detected in the blood. But, these antibodies mean only that a person has been infected with the AIDS virus at some time. Their presence does not mean the person is still infected. The test for AIDS virus antibodies is used to screen donated blood and plasma. This process should help to eliminate the transmission of the AIDS virus through blood and blood products. The test for AIDS virus antibodies is available through private physicians and most state or local health departments.

As we said before, AIDS does not actually kill anyone. It opens up the body to infection by other diseases. About 85 percent of patients with the AIDS virus die from one or both of two rather rare diseases. One is a type of cancer known as Kaposi's sarcoma (KS). KS occurs anywhere on the surface of the skin or in the mouth. It begins with a spot which looks like a bruise, either blue-violet or brownish in color. As KS develops, the spots grow larger and spread to other parts or organs of the body. The other rare disease associated with AIDS is Pneumocystis carinii pneumonia (PCP). This is a parasitic infection of the lungs and has symptoms which include cough, fever and difficulty in breathing.

We should again stress that there is absolutely *no danger* of contracting AIDS from donating blood. There is always a tremendous need for blood. People who have not been infected with the AIDS virus and are not among the high risk groups should continue to donate blood as they have in the past.

PREVENTION

AIDS can be prevented. The use of HTLV—III antibody screening tests at blood donor sites reduces the risk. Prevention is also enhanced when members of high risk groups voluntarily refrain from donating blood for medical use. There is no vaccine for AIDS itself. The only way for members of high risk groups, homosexual men and abusers of intravenous drugs, to keep from getting the disease is to avoid sexual activity and the abuse of drugs with dirty or shared needles. The Public Health Service recommends that the following steps be taken to prevent the spread of AIDS:

— Do not have sexual contact with people known or suspected of having AIDS.
— Do not have sex with multiple partners, or with persons who have had multiple partners.
— Persons who are at increased risk for having AIDS should not donate blood.
— Physicians should order blood transfusions for patients only when medically necessary.
— Health workers should use extreme care when handling or disposing of contaminated hypodermic needles.
— Don't abuse IV drugs; if you use IV drugs, don't share needles or syringes (boiling does not guarantee sterility).
— Don't have sex with people who abuse IV drugs.
— Don't use inhalant nitrites (poppers); their role as a cofactor for Kaposi's sarcoma is being investigated.

People with positive HTLV—III antibody tests should take these precautions as well:

— A regular medical evaluation and follow-up is advised.
— Do not donate blood, plasma, body organs, other tissue or sperm.
— Take precautions against exchanging body fluids during sexual activity.
— There is a risk of infecting others by sexual intercourse, sharing of needles, and possibly, exposure of others to your saliva through oral-genital contact or intimate kissing (the effectiveness of condoms in preventing infection with HTLV—III is not proved, but their consistent use may reduce transmission, since exchange of body fluids is known to increase risk).
— Toothbrushes, razors or other implements that could become contaminated with blood should not be shared.

— Women whose sexual partner is antibody positive are themselves at increased risk of acquiring AIDS. If they become pregnant, their children are also at increased risk of acquiring AIDS.

Special thanks to the Public Health Service of the U.S. Department of Health and Human Services for this information on AIDS. The Public Health Service AIDS hotline number is 1-800-447-AIDS. Atlanta area callers should dial (409) 329-1295.

In spite of this information, the warnings and the fear about the spread of AIDS, the disease will continue to infect more and more people. One of the reasons for this is that while medical doctors and researchers warn against sexual activity among the high risk groups, others persist in encouraging unrestrained gratification of sexual lust.

One of the most famous and visible of these is Dr. Ruth Westheimer. In her best-selling book, *Guide to Good Sex*, she advises male homosexuals to have casual sex in bathhouses, preaches that pornography and swallowing semen are completely harmless, instructs some men to hire prostitute lovers and teaches teenagers how to sodomize their boyfriends. When Dr. Ruth was asked about AIDS she said she couldn't comment because she is not a physician! Yet the very activity which she condones, teaches and encourages has been proven to contribute to the spread of AIDS. That is *not* good sex! It certainly is not God-pleasing sex, but a terrible twisting and perverting of this wonderful gift of God to married couples.

One very frightening thing about AIDS is that it didn't even exist, or at least wasn't known to man, before 1970. AIDS is a product of our current society. The 60s, 70s and 80s have been the age of tolerance for anything by anybody. It is the age of overindulgence. We fear to "impose" our social and religious values on anyone else with the result that we eventually lose our own values. We have trivialized sex. Early teenage and pre-teenage sex have become commonplace. It is an age of anticelibacy. Homosexuals have come out of the closet. The practice of homosexuality has become almost acceptable to those who once found it intolerable. As a result of this casual attitude toward sex, we have become a society characterized by easy, irresponsible sex, abortion on demand, genital herpes and AIDS.

Dr. George Lundberg, editor of the Journal of the American Medical Association, asserts that AIDS is one of the greatest health threats in the history of man. He classifies AIDS with the historical scourges of syphilis among the Spanish, the plague among the French, tuberculosis among Alaska's Eskimos and smallpox among the American Indians.

Yet where does the money go with regard to AIDS? Is it spent to stop the spread of this deadly disease? Is it spent to enforce many of the already existing laws that would greatly hinder the transmission of AIDS? No, instead money is being spent on research for a cure and a vaccine — a vaccine that will allow the high risk groups to continue their lives of sinful wantonness and lust. Anyone who suggests that the focus on AIDS should shift from finding a vaccine to changing the sinful lifestyles or stopping the dangerous behavior which puts people at risk is classified as an unloving, uncaring hypocritical religious fanatic.

NBC recently broadcast a special on AIDS which began by intimating that religion is part of the evil which prevents a cure and vaccine for AIDS. The beginning of the program, entitled *"AIDS — Fear and Fact,"* was a condemnation of a very religious family for throwing out of their home their homosexual son with AIDS. The implication was that religious people do not care about the victims of AIDS. At the same time, the homosexual community of San Francisco was praised for the precautions it has taken to make the practice of homosexuality safe and for their cooperation and support of AIDS victims. Yet an undeniable fact remains: there would be little or no spread of the disease called AIDS as we know it in our country today if the biblical injunctions concerning sexual activity and sobriety were followed.

It is up to Christians to declare the law of God in all its harsh severity against the practice of homosexuality or any other sin. Unrepented sin can only lead to eternal death. We shall also share the sweet saving gospel to bring some to repentance and life, remembering that God punished Jesus for all our sins — the sins of the homosexual and the sins of the world. "Look, the Lamb of God, who takes away the sin of the world!" (John 1:24) "He is the atoning sacrifice for our sins, and not only for ours but also for the sins of the whole world" (1 John 2:2).

SOLI DEO GLORIA

NOTES

1. Heron, Ann, editor. *One Teenager in Ten.* Boston: Alyson Publications, 1983, pp. 19-20.
2. *Ibid.*, pp. 29-31.
3. *Ibid.*, pp. 13-14.
4. Plass, Ewald M., editor. *What Luther Says.* St. Louis: Concordia Publishing House, 1959, p. 134.
5. *Ibid.*
6. *Ibid.*, p. 1304.
7. *Ibid.*, p. 1269.
8. "D & D Takes Position on Homosexuality." *Christian News Encyclopedia.* Vol. II. Washington, MO: Missourian Publishing Company, 1983, p. 1015.
9. Hunter, Barbara J. "Homosexuality and the Church — a Perspective from Paul and Romans 14:1-12." Student Paper for New Testament Ethics and Theology. Columbus: Trinity Lutheran Seminary, 1984.

APPENDIX 1.

World News (from *The Concord*)

LOMA LINDA, CALIF. — Closed-couple gay relationships should be encouraged for gay Seventh-Day Adventists, according to Loma Linda University biblical ethics professor David Larson. In an article in the May 1984 issue of *Spectrum*, Larson went on to say that Christians must stop accusing the sexually-different of "perversion."

NEW YORK — The New York State Supreme Court declared New York City Mayor Ed Koch's order barring city-funded agencies from discriminating against gay people unconstitutional, and could threaten other executive orders protecting gay job rights in New York state. The court challenge was brought by the Roman Catholic Archdiocese of New York, the Salvation Army, and Agudath Israel of America. (from the *Bay Area Reporter*)

NEW YORK — A research study by the State University of New York suggests that male homosexuality may have its origins in "biological markers."

The complete study, released in the Sept. 28, 1984 *Science Magazine* (Vol. 225), states that "the secretory pattern of luteinizing hormone in the homosexuals in response to estrogen was intermediate between that of the heterosexual men and that of the women. Furthermore, testosterone was depressed for a significantly longer period in the homosexual men than in the heterosexual men. These findings suggest that biological markers for sexual orientation may exist." Further, the study stated that, "This invites the idea that there may be physiological developmental components in the sexual orientation of some homosexual men."

CINCINNATI — The Presbyterian Church (USA) has asked the federal appeals court to hold that a Louisville bank violated the 1964 Civil Rights Act when it fired a branch manager who told his supervisors that he was president of a group of lesbian and gay Roman Catholics and Episcopalians.

SAN FRANCISCO — The National Board of Lutherans Concerned/North America met in the bay city at the same time as the Lesbian/Gay Interfaith Alliance held its second annual meeting (Oct. 12-14). Under the theme "Strategies for a New Vision," the Alliance held a day of workshops and an interfaith prayer service open to the public; business meetings were restricted to delegates to the national organization. (from the LC/Los Angeles newsletter)

BOSTON, BERKELEY — A resolution of "openness to and affirmation of gay, lesbian and bisexual persons" in the United Church of Christ, was adopted at the recent annual meeting of its Massachusetts Conference, according to the national Office of Communication for the denomination.

The resolution was also adopted at the fourth National Gathering of the United Church Coalition for Lesbian/Gay Concerns at its meeting in Berkeley, California.

The National Gathering urged other U.C.C. Conferences to pass similar resolutions in preparation for the 1985 General Synod. (from the LC/Los Angeles newsletter)

PHOENIX — James Andrews, formerly the Stated Clerk of the Presbyterian Church (US) and recently elected Stated Clerk of the merged Presbyterian Church (USA), has indicated that he believes that Presbyterians have not seriously practiced what they preached in regard to supporting gay civil rights and in welcoming gay men and lesbians into the church as members. He has expressed his own commitment to remedy this failure of the church. (from the Evangelicals Concerned newsletter, *Record*)

NEW YORK — The National Council of Churches (NCCC) Executive Committee concurred with the opinion of a special NCCC Governing Board's vote in November 1983 to "postpone indefinitely the vote on eligibility for consideration for membership of the Universal Fellowship of Metropolitan Community Churches (UFMCC) was "in effect an indirect rejection of the main motion."

The application of the UFMCC, which has a particular ministry to homosexuals, will remain on file with the NCCC. However, the UFMCC would need to update its application and "request in writing that the application be reactivated" in order for the application to become the subject of further consideration by the Governing Board, the committee ruled. The committee's opinion also will be reported to the NCCC's November 1984 Governing Board meeting in New Brunswick, NJ, for its concurrence. (from the LC/Los Angeles Newsletter)

NORTHRIDGE, CALIF. — By a unanimous vote of congregational ballot, St. Paul's Lutheran Church (LCA) approved the affirmation of Welcome of LC/NA's Reconciled-in-Christ project, which seeks congregations that welcome gay and lesbian Christians as full and equal members of the Body of Christ.

Pacific Southwest Synod (LCA) Bishop Stanley Olson, attending the congregation after the vote was taken, congratulated the church and lauded them on their commitment to the unconditional Gospel.

BALTIMORE — The National Conference of Catholic Charities adopted a resolution on homosexuals which read in part: "Be it resolved . . . that the NCC movement take on a prophetic role by committing itself to an educational effort to help people become sensitive to the social trauma suffered by people with a gay orientation." (from the Evangelicals Concerned newsletter, *Record*)

SAN FRANCISCO — Mayor Diane Feinstein rejected the year-long study of the task force on a "domestic partners" health benefits plan out-of-hand, before it had been formally presented to her. Mayor Feinstein claimed the panel "had strayed too far from its original mandate" to consider the effects of benefits for any designated beneficiary of a city worker. The panel felt that approach to be too broad and financially unfeasible, and suggested that focus be shifted to "domestic partners" of gay and lesbian city workers. Feinstein rejected that notion emphatically. Supervisor Harry Britt was also uncomfortable with the recommendation, which he felt ought to extend to partners of non-gay as well as gay/lesbian workers. (from the *Bay Area Reporter*)

APPENDIX 2.

Reconciled-in-Christ

An energetic and vital Reconciled-in-Christ program has been assembled and put into operation by Lutherans Concerned in order to reach Lutheran congregations on a global basis. Many gay and lesbian Lutherans remain within their congregations, rather than leaving their parishes to join churches having a special ministry to gay/lesbian people. What the Reconciled-in-Christ program seeks to accomplish is to identify Lutheran congregations engaged in ministry inclusive of lesbian and gay people. Also, it gives an opportunity for congregations to show their love and concern for lesbian and gay Lutherans.

A congregation may ask, "All people are welcome here; why should we single out gay people?"

The Reconciled-in-Christ program doesn't seek special treatment for gay people. It simply seeks to make clearer the policy of the church that all people are welcome as full members, regardless of affectional orientation. Moreover, making a clear affirmation can be an important part of evangelism — bringing the Good News to all people.

What will happen if we participate?

A congregation can join the program by having its council approve the Program's "Affirmation of Welcome." This document is then sent to the national offices of Lutherans Concerned, which maintains a roster of participating congregations. The roster will be publicized appropriately for the purpose of letting gay and lesbian people know they are welcome in your congregation.

What is the Affirmation of Welcome?

The Affirmation of Welcome is a statement that affirms the message of Christ that calls us to reconciliation and wholeness. Since gay and lesbian persons are often scorned by society and alienated from the Church, the affirmation states the following:

*that gay and lesbian people share with all others the worth that comes from being unique individuals created by God;

*that gay and lesbian people are welcome within the membership of this congegation upon making the same affirmation of faith that all other people make; and

*that as members of this congregation, gay and lesbian people are expected and encouraged to share in the sacramental and general life of this congregation.

What churches have affirmed God's unconditional Gospel?

St. Paul's LCA, Oakland, California
St. Francis ALC, San Francisco, California
University LCA, Palo Alto, California
St. Mark's LCA, San Francisco, California
First United LCA, San Francisco, California
St. Paulus AELC, San Francisco, California
St. Paul's LCA, Northridge, California
St. Paul-Reformation LCA, St. Paul, Minnesota
Resurrection LCA, Chicago, Illinois
St. Gregory of Nyssa AELC, Chicago, Illinois

GLOSSARY OF HOMOSEXUAL TERMS

Baths — Special baths frequented by homosexuals when looking for sex. Gang sex often occurs in such places.

Bisexual — One who has sexual relations with both sexes.

Butch — A masculine or super-masculine homosexual. Many wear boots, leather clothing, or extremely tight-fitting clothing that show off their muscles and emphasize their genitalia.

Chicken — A young homosexual.

Chicken Hawk — An older homosexual who seeks to pick up a "chicken."

Closet Gay — A homosexual who, for personal or professional reasons, hides or covers his homosexuality.

Cruise — A sexually stimulated homosexual out looking for a partner. Often a homosexual who is cruising will advertise his preference by wearing a handkerchief in his hip pocket. Anything on the left means the man wants to do the act; anything on the right means he wants to receive it.

blue: anal intercourse	olive: military
black: Sado-masochism	orange: wants to do anything — supposedly
brown: feces	red: fist intercourse
green: money, a hustler	yellow: urine

grey: bondage   white: masturbation, usually im-
                                plies mutual

Drag — Female clothes worn by a male to impersonate a female.

Drag Queen — A queen dressed in drag on the prowl.

Faggot — The stereotyped homosexual; a limp-wristed, femi-
nine acting homosexual often looked down upon by other
homosexuals.

Fellatio — The practice of obtaining sexual satisfaction (or-
gasm) by oral stimulation of the penis.

Gay — Favorite term of the homosexual community to describe
themselves.

Gay Bars — The places in which gays congregate for dancing,
pickups and sexual contacts.

Golden Showers/Water Sports — Activity involving urine for
sexual gratification.

Heterosexual — Those who confine their sexual activity to
members of the opposite sex.

Homosexual — A man or woman who engages in sexual activity with another member of the same sex. Such activity
usually leads to an orgasmic experience.

Hustler — a male prostitute.

Latent Homosexual — A cruel and harmful term (attributed to
Sigmund Freud) suggesting that some people are born with
homosexual tendencies. Many people believe that men who
use effeminate gestures and mannerisms or women who act
masculine possess "latent homosexual tendencies." This is
a lie. Studies show that over 80 percent of the "effeminate"
acting men and "masculine" women are heterosexual.

Lesbian — A woman homosexual. She usually brings her female partner to sexual climax by manipulation of the
clitoris with either her finger or tongue. They sometimes
spell women as "womyn" to distinguish them from heterosexual women.

Old Queen — An old, effeminate homosexual male, usually no
longer desirable as a sex partner, who often experiences
extreme loneliness and has the highest unhappiness quo-
tient and suicide rate.

Pseudosexual — A person who possesses certain superficial characteristics that cause people to erroneously label them homosexual when in reality they are not.

Queen — An effeminate male homosexual (also called nelly or fairy).

Sadist and Masochist, or "Slave Master" — One who adds brutality or cruelty, either physical or mental, to sexuality. Some punish their partners; others prefer to be punished or tortured themselves.

Sodomy — Anal intercourse between persons.

Straight — A heterosexual person.

Transvestite — A person who likes to wear one or more pieces of clothing of the opposite sex. Contrary to popular opinion, most of these people remain heterosexual, marry, and raise a family (if the spouse can overlook this idiosyncrasy).

Trouble — Butch that may cause trouble or is dangerous.